Moving to Learn

Moving to Learn

A Guide to
Psychomotor
Development
in Early
Childhood

Diane Nyisztor

Eva Stelzer Rudick

VANIER COLLEGE

HARCOURT
BRACE
CANADA

Harcourt Brace & Company, Canada
Toronto Montreal Fort Worth New York Orlando
Philadelphia San Diego London Sydney Tokyo

Canadian Cataloguing in Publication Data
Nyisztor, Diane
        Moving to learn: a guide to psychomotor
development in early childhood
Includes bibliographical references and index.
ISBN 0-7747-3356-X

1. Perceptual-motor learning. 2. Motor ability
in children. I. Rudick, Eva Stelzer. II. Title.

LB1067. N95 1994   370.15'5   C94-932131-1

Publisher: *Heather McWhinney*
Editor and Marketing Manager: *Joanna Cotton*
Projects Co-ordinator: *Laura Paterson Pratt*
Director of Publishing Services: *Jean Davies*
Editorial Manager: *Marcel Chiera*
Production Manager: *Sue-Ann Becker*
Production Supervisor: *Carol Tong*
Copy Editor: *Gail Marsden*
Cover Design: *Opus House*
Interior Photography: *Debbie Becker Newpol*
Cover Photography: *Brett Lamb*
Printing and Binding: *Webcom Limited*

This book was printed in Canada on acid-free paper.

1 2 3 4 5   99 98 97 96 95

PREFACE

Moving to Learn is a practical guide for Early Childhood Educators, Physical Educators, and Students preparing to work with or already working with children from birth to twelve years of age. Whether you are working with infants in the day care environment or with school age children in an extended day setting, this book will be valuable to you. There are many publications on the market today that deal with the theory of motor development and many that provide movement based activities. So, why is this book different? It introduces theory at a comprehensive level followed by practical and developmentally appropriate movement opportunities that corroborate the theory. These *learning opportunities* are placed in a format that can easily be transferred to index cards and used to complement whatever curricular model you choose to use. For example, some opportunities might be selected for use by topic, such as Spring, while others might be selected based on the fundamental skill they develop.

Our practical and formal training resulted in a subtle change in our approach to movement education over the years. These resulting ideas provided the impetus to write a book that stresses the need for a positive approach and the provision of developmentally appropriate opportunities to move the body for the sake of pleasure, fitness, skill development, and skill refinement. We also believe that in western culture, self-esteem is closely linked to the way in which we perceive our bodies. As educators we are in a position to foster this self-esteem by providing appropriate learning opportunities.

Moving to Learn focuses on the development of the child's psychomotor domain, how the child begins to move, and how these movements influence and impact on the development of the whole child. Each chapter provides a theoretical base for discussion, followed by practical examples that we refer to as Learning Opportunities. Movement is both a learned and maturational process. This text looks at the way in which the infant, toddler, pre-school, and school age child learns by moving through the environment and how information is taken in through these movements. We look at a combination of understanding the stages of motor development, perceptual development, and effective planning that will help you provide children with the greatest learning through movement.

We see children as natural movers and shakers who are anxious to learn about their environment. They must be provided with opportunities to go into their environment and retrieve information for themselves. Knowledge about ourselves and how our body functions is not limited to the psychomotor domain but is part of an active process of learning and is the foundation of our book.

The practitioner will need an understanding of theory in order to provide appropriate opportunities for each child. The diagrams, figures, and checklists have been developed over many years of teaching. Class discussion would often lead to pictorial representations of ideas. This formed the basis of many of the figures and diagrams. Sequencing for presenting skills evolved from our own trial and error experiences. Children's drawings were provided by children under ten years of age who were asked to represent any idea related to physical activity. We have not altered their pictures in any way as we feel it is special to see a child's perspective. We have tried wherever possible to use straight forward and simple language.

The book is divided into three parts. Part I provides the general framework and looks at children and their bodies. In Chapter 1 we highlight the importance of using observations as a basis for planning. We provide checklists throughout this book and devote a section that explains both the purpose of observations and how to use the checklists that we have designed. Chapter 2 focuses on *perceptual motor development*, and the idea that both internal and external stimuli support learning. We also believe in the concept of a feedback system as a means of taking in and processing information. Chapter 3 looks at the underlying principles of balance and health-related aspects of physical fitness.

In Part II, we look at a developmental perspective examining the milestones of children's movements as well as self initiated actions. We discuss stages of motor development, beginning with the newborn infant's involuntary actions or reflexes and including an introduction to the rudiments of voluntary action. Chapter 5 and 6 discuss purposeful controlled movements, known as fundamental movements. Chapter 7 looks at the schoolage child. It deals with the refinement and combination of fundamental movement patterns required for specific sports-related and dance skills.

Part III includes an overview of how to apply the relevant theory in planning and selecting opportunities that support a developmentally appropriate curriculum design. This section is meant to assist the practitioner, student teacher, or parent, who confronted with the children in their care, says "*What Now?*". Our intention here is to expand the general concepts discussed earlier in the text. Chapter 8 takes a detailed look at planning a psychomotor setup in terms of the environment, self selected play opportunities, teacher directed situations and team teaching. Chapter 9 examines nonelimination in both a cooperative and cognitively appropriate competitive context. Chapter 10 provides ideas for parachute play. Both Chapter's 9 and 10 deal with the social relations between children and decisions that children make from within. Motor activities can help children work with and learn from each other. Children are asked to find solutions to movement games. This can only be achieved through the development of interpersonal relations. Children will also need to look within themselves in order to decide what they want to or can do to make a particular situation work. Chapter 11 looks at creative movement as the root of creative dance and a means to furthering an understanding of perceptual motor development. Through creative movement we develop a greater understanding of ourselves as we learn to work from within.

Appendix A provides a guide to assist in understanding developmentally appropriate planning. In Appendix B we have used the guidelines of Appendix A to situate our learning opportunities. Appendix B also provides a quick identification of what developmental, perceptual motor, and fitness areas each learning opportunity fits under. Appendix C provides sources for purchase of related material and equipment. An extensive glossary and index are provided as tools to assist the reader. Each chapter ends with learning opportunities that can be easily adapted to any teaching situation.

To facilitate the writing process, we have decided to interchange the pronouns he and she in alternating chapters.

We have tried and tested all of the learning opportunities, checklists, and sequences for skill presentation that are provided throughout this book. Many of the ideas we present we have been doing for so long that we are unsure at times when they became ours. We would therefore like to thank everyone who contributed to our ideas, especially the children we have worked with, as many of our concepts evolved from them. We invite you to use them in whatever way meets your program needs in order to help plan a developmentally appropriate program that will meet the physical needs of your children.

ACKNOWLEDGEMENTS

Many people helped make this book possible. Molly's quick eye and feedback sent us thinking and correcting. Irene Christie was there both at the first and last. Debbie Becker Newpol devoted time and photographic skills. Joanna Cotton provided moral support and made this work a reality. Laura Paterson Pratt carefully read many versions of our chapters and Jean Monpetit and Grace Edeh tested versions of the manuscript with their students. Valuable comments and suggestions were provided by reviewers: Paulette Cote-Laurence, Brock University; Scott MacKinnon, Mount St. Vincent University; and Connie Winder, George Brown College. Thanks to the many students who used versions of the work, for without them, there would be no need for such a book.

SPECIAL MENTION

No book is written alone. This one is no exception. Many people played an important role in permitting me to complete this work. Firstly, I would like to thank my three children, Joelle, Elana, and Lauren, for their unlimited patience and understanding. They often had to try out learning opportunities in order to assess the accuracy of the directions as they were written. They had to endure many nights of pizza suppers (not such a difficult task). Mostly, they showed the kind of pride in my achievement that is normally reserved for parents toward their children. A special thank you to my husband Gerry who never complained through my endless hours of work. He always believed I could complete this task, even when it seemed to me impossible.

Thanks to Scott Gardiner for his invaluable critique during a time when this book was merely an idea, to Moses Schwartz and Momi Ben-Shach who provided invaluable technological knowledge and assistance.

Last, but not least, I would like to thank my co-author Diane for being so wonderful to work with, for understanding me when I was too many steps ahead, and for becoming my friend in the process of our work.

Eva Stelzer Rudick

––

The writing of this book would have been impossible if it had not been for the support of so many individuals. To Eva, I want to thank her for believing in me. She provided me with the encouragement that was necessary to start writing this book and the determination to complete it!

To my mother, who is always there for me and does so much. Her help provided me with the time I needed to pursue this goal.

To my husband who not only supported my efforts but was there every step of the way helping me to master the computer, which was essential in the completion of this book.

And last but not least, I would like to thank my children Michael and Jessica who were very patient and tried to be understanding during the creation of this book.

Diane Nyisztor

––

A NOTE FROM THE PUBLISHER

Thank you for selecting <u>Moving To Learn</u> by Diane Nyisztor and Eva Stelzer Rudick. The authors and publisher have devoted considerable time to the careful development of this book. We appreciate your recognition of this effort and accomplishment.

We want to hear what you think about <u>Moving to Learn</u>. Please take a few minutes to fill in the stamped student reply card at the back of the book. Your comments and suggestions will be valuable to us as we prepare new editions and other books.

TABLE OF CONTENTS

PART I

CHILDREN AND THEIR BODIES

Chapter 1

In this chapter you will learn about:

- Learning to move and moving to learn
  - principles of motor development
  - exploring the environment
  - cephalocaudal development
  - proximodistal development
- Using observations
- Increasing each child's potential

INTRODUCTION

LEARNING TO MOVE AND MOVING TO LEARN

Learning to Move: Principles of Motor Development

Learning to move can be explained as the process of developing "control of self movements" (Keogh and Sugden, 1985, p. 247). Control of self movements refers to the increasing motor control individuals have over their bodies. We will refer to this increase in motor control as **motor development**. This development and the rate of motor skill acquisition is guided in part by genetic makeup and is rather sequential in nature. Although the rate of development varies slightly, children generally go through the same developmental process in the very same sequence (Piaget and Inhelder, 1969, Cratty, 1986). The *Law of Developmental Direction* and *Differentiation* describes **cephalocaudal** and **proximodistal** development and **motor refinement**. The word cephalocaudal stems from the Latin word *cephal* meaning head and refers to a process whereby infants first gain control of their upper body, such as the head and neck. This control then moves down to the trunk and limbs. Proximodistal development is a process whereby infants first gain control of the centre of their body. This control then develops outward toward the extremities. Proximal stems from the root words *proximal* meaning near and *distal* meaning far. Motor refinement describes the progression of development from the large muscles of the body to the smaller muscles leadning to more refined movements.

Some children, as stated earlier, will spend longer at one stage of development than another. The same is true for the acquisition of motor skills. For example, most children learn to catch a ball. Some may spend longer at the immature stage of catching while others may progress quickly to the mature stage. Ultimately, each child achieves a certain degree of proficiency towards the **fundamental skill** of catching but each one's genetic makeup and previous experience dictates that they will master certain skills at a different rate. We will refer to this previous experience on which to input new information as a foundation for **knowledge based** learning.

Moving to Learn: Exploring the Environment

Moving to learn can be described as "moving in relation to changing conditions" (Keogh and Sugden, 1985, p. 247). It involves the interrelationship between perception, sensorimotor learning, and the environment. We will refer to this interrelationship as **perceptualmotor development**. Sensorimotor here refers to the relationship between information taken in by the senses in the form of stimuli, movement that is used to seek out this stimuli, and the movement that it produces. It is a combination of sensory perceptions and physical actions (Gardner, 1993). Moving to learn is affected by the environment. It is in this area that an instructor can be extremely effective. How a movement program is designed will inevitably influence motor learning. We see physical and motor learning as an interactive process involving the child, developmental stages, the educator, and the environment. Children learn everywhere. Moving through and manipulating objects in the environment provide endless opportunity to learn through hands-on experiences. You also have the potential to inspire children to develop perceptualmotor concepts of body, spatial, temporal, and directional awareness and to provide experiences that will enhance visual, auditory, and tactile perception. Once you acquire the theoretical foundation of motor development you can provide an array of developmentally appropriate movement opportunities to enhance balance and to increase health and physical fitness and the fundamental skills of locomotion, nonlocomotion, and manipulation.

Moving to learn expands movement potential through motor opportunities and enables us to learn about other concepts through movement. For example, we learn vocabulary by verbally reinforcing actions as we see them and by talking about the texture of a movement, such as it being fast or slow. Performance of motor ability is improved as we repeat a motor action. The cues that help us carry out a task require less visual attention and external feedback. Actions become internalized, the need for feedback is reduced, and we begin to rely on internal control(Holding,1989).

Different theorists distinguish the domains differently. A good curriculum model involves an understanding of each domain where the educational objectives target the whole child. This book is presented from the perspective of the psychomotor domain. It is worthy of note that we do not see the psychomotor domain in isolation, but that we subscribe to the holistic view and the interrelationship among all domains. These may be classified for the purpose of educational objectives into the psychomotor, cognitive, social, and affective domains. As Simpson (1972) aptly points out these were designed to assist in writing educational objectives and were not meant as classifications of behaviours.

Perception is a cognitive skill and as such we regard perceptual motor development as the marriage of mind and body. Piaget (in Cratty, 1986) was the first to explain the relationship between problem solving and intelligence. He was responsible for the groundwork to the idea that intelligence has its foundation in certain elementary perceptual and motor functions(Piaget, 1966). Gardner (1983) expands on this idea by saying that "intellectual competence must entail a set of skills of problem solving - enabling the individual to resolve genuine problems or difficulties that he or she encounters"(1983, p.60). *So what does this mean to the educator?*

Firstly, all movements take place in the psychomotor domain through what Gardner refers to as body kinaesthetic ability. Psychomotor tasks can be developmental, life sustaining, or for recreation, pleasure, or financial gain as in competitive sport (Harrow, 1972). Secondly, movements can be used to explore the world around. Through movement we can participate in the cognitive domain and the social and affective domain. When children move they are learning about the potential of their bodies and about the environment around them. You are in a position to provide opportunity for children to use their bodies to increase knowledge about themselves and the world around them. This happens not independently of, but concurrently, with the body's natural development. We see an interrelationship between the maturationist view and the use of movement to increase knowledge. Gardner (1983) classifies intelligence into seven categories. These multiple intelligences include *musical, spatial, body kinaesthetic, linguistic, logical mathematical, interpersonal, and intrapersonal intelligence.* He discusses movement in primarily the body kinaesthetic area. This does not conflict with the holistic view we subscribe to in early childhood education. Body kinaesthetic intelligence occurs when you express yourself physically and perform motor functions. These actions are part of the psychomotor domain. Through movement, learning occurs in other areas. For example, in cooperative and group games we must work together to solve problems, relate to one another to ensure success, thereby developing interpersonal and intrapersonal intelligence, which take place in the socioaffective domain. Through creative movement we become involved in cognitive functions, developing an understanding of perceptual relations of space, time, and direction. We also use physical language to express feeling and emotions within. There are times when we move in pairs or groups, developing interpersonal skills of the social and affective domain. Musical intelligence, according to Gardner, addresses auditory perception, rhythm, and listening skills, many of the skills needed for dance and creative movement. These skills overlap in the cognitive and socioaffective domain. Solving problems through movement is a cognitive skill and problem solving is an important factor in increasing intelligence (Piaget, 1966, Gardner, 1983).

Self-initiated actions occur most naturally in a well constructed play environment. You can successfully provide wonderful opportunities for learning through movement and sensorimotor experiences by creating and setting up appropriate learning environments for gross motor play, sensorimotor, and fine motor experiences. Strive to provide holistic activities that require components from each of the domains.

Gross motor play provides opportunities for children to master movements and discover information. Fine motor play will provide opportunity to develop muscles in the fingers and hands. Tactile information can be gathered through fine motor experiences. Learning in tactile experiences occurs through sensorimotor exploration. "The younger the children, the more dependant they are on sensory learning and physical contact with their environment in order to learn and to know." (Shipley, 1993, p.16) Children aged seven through twelve, which we refer to as the middle years, should still be provided with many ways to use their bodies physically. There are many games with rules, for example, that can assist the school age child in developing thinking and problem solving skills, while stimulating motor and physical fitness. When working with school age children, it is important that you pay particular attention to keeping motor activities fun and challenging in order to maintain a high level of motivation. Focus on increasing the level of physical fitness, an area often neglected in the school child's sedentary day. Ensure that enough time is devoted to sport, dance, sport-related tasks, and forms of creative expression. The next section examines the components involved in using observations of children to help plan a developmentally appropriate curriculum. We refer you to Appendix A as well.

USING OBSERVATIONS

Preparation and planning of a developmentally appropriate movement program requires three essential components: an understanding of the theoretical framework, observations, and planning ideas. There exists a very important and strong link between the knowledge of a topic, observations, and planning. Anecdotal reports and checklists can be successfully used to strengthen observations and apply practical meaning to theoretical knowledge. Following is an introduction to the use of checklists in this text. A more detailed discussion of planning based on observations is found in Chapter 8.

As educators we spend a considerable amount of our day observing children. These observations, whether informal, or formal provide us with essential information about the children we are working with. In order to plan effectively it is essential that you allocate sufficient time for observing to gather information on the children. You have all spent time observing children in a variety of situations whether it be in the dramatic play area as the doctor bandages his patients or on the playground as they climb a rope or ride their tricycles. As safety is often a concern during outdoor play much of your observation time is devoted to ensuring the safety of the children. In so doing you also observe how the children use the equipment and the material. You observe which children spend their time climbing and which children prefer to play in the sand box.

These checklists are meant to facilitate the process of observations and to help you determine which skills have been mastered by the children in your group and which ones they are still working on. Use the checklists in the format that is most beneficial to you. Depending on the checklist you may choose to either observe one child in all the skills listed or you might prefer to observe all children in one specific skill.

Your observations will assist you in recognizing certain developmental milestones and determining what will occur next. We recommend the following format for utilizing the checklists.

STEP 1

Spend at least five minutes per observation. Watch the children as they play in their environment. The younger the group of children, the more frequent the observations should be. Repeat observations on a regular basis, as changes in physical development occur rapidly in the early years. Vary the settings or circumstances under which the observations are carried out.

Place a check mark, along with the date of observation, next to each developmental milestone as it is observed.

STEP 2

The checklists are designed to provide the reader with two categorizations of information. First it will give a profile of the child's movement capability and second it will identify the abilities the child has not yet achieved.

Learning opportunities should be designed, selected, or made available based on these observations.

Provide a combination of opportunities to encourage further growth and development to practice already acquired skills.

STEP 3

Once Steps 1 and 2 have been completed, assess and modify the learning opportunities presented in this book and both use and/or adjust them according to your needs. Learning opportunities from other books, courses, and, of course, your own experiences should be incorporated into the curriculum.

Too often observations are used as assessments of the children instead of assessments of the curriculum. We suggest that the data obtained through the use of the checklists be used to help you develop goals and objectives for your movement program. These goals and program objectives will provide you with the direction necessary in designing a sound and developmentally appropriate curriculum. After all, *if you don't know where you are going, how will you get there?*

INCREASING EACH CHILD'S POTENTIAL

Regardless of what you set out to achieve, the movement opportunities you provide should ensure that experiences are directed to the child's current level of development. It is important to plan an environment rich in opportunity for children to move just for the sake of moving, to touch for the sake of their own curiosity, and to generally explore with no intended product. Focus on the process! Enough time should be provided for children to explore and develop their own understanding of the skills and concepts involved in what they are doing. Even if the child has mastered a particular skill he should still be given the opportunity and encouraged to practise in those areas as more exposure to a given task will result in refinement of that skill. Emphasis should not be placed on the achievement of a perfected skill or on winning a game. Rather concentrate on each individual's skills and on each person's own potential for growth through movement oriented experiences. We also recommend that you plan learning opportunities from simple to complex. This idea is developed within various chapters of the text.

Physical ability is strongly linked to an individual's sense of self and positive motor experiences lead to a positive self-image. "Young children form their body image through activity.....Gradually they build up an idea of the relationship of their body to the space around them."(Nash, 1989, p.143)

Children should derive pleasure from exploration of the materials as well as from moving different parts of their bodies in different ways. Varying the materials and the way in which they are presented will stimulate the child and help to maintain a high interest level. Children will only pursue what is interesting to them and they should be motivated to set their own challenges. After all, children do not usually have the same goals and objectives that we have. You may want to provide experiences with a main objective of improving a child's ability to throw an object accurately at a target. The child will more probably be concerned that the experiences are interesting enough to spend time on. More than likely, the child's goal will not be to perfect the skill of throwing but to pursue something that is pleasurable.

CHAPTER HIGHLIGHTS

Learning to move is a developmental process. Moving to learn depends on exploration of the environment to enhance learning. Cephalocaudal development refers to the developmental process of acquiring control over the body from the head down to the toe. Proximodistal development refers to the development that occurs first in the trunk region and progresses outward to the extremities. Refinement refers to mastering first gross motor, then fine motor, skills.

Observations play an important role in the foundation of a sound and individualized curriculum.

REFERENCES

Cratty, Bryant J. (1986) *Perceptual and Motor Development in Infants and Children.* Englewood Cliffs, New Jersey: Prentice-Hall.

Gardner, Howard (1983) *Frames of Mind.* New York: Basic Books.

Gardner, Howard (1993) *Frames of Mind,* anniversary edition, Basic Books.

Goleman, Daniel, Kaufman, Paul, and Ray Michael (1992) *The Creative Spirit.* New York: Penguin.

Harrow, Anita J. (1972) *A Taxonomy of the Psychomotor Domain.* New York: David McKay Company.

Hendrick, Joanne (1990) *Total Learning.* 3rd edition. New York: MacMillan Publishing Company.

Holding, Dennis H. (1989) *Human Skills.* New York: John Wiley and Sons.

Keogh, Jack and Sugden, David (1985) *Movement Skill Development.* New York: MacMillan Publishing Company.

Lazlo, Judith I. and Bairstow, Phillip J. (1985) *Perceptual-Motor Behaviour, Developmental Assessment and Therapy.* Great Britain: Holt, Rinehart, & Winston.

Nash, Chris (1989) *The Learning Environment, A Practical Approach to the Education of the Three, Four, and Five Year Old.* Canada: Collier MacMillan.

Piaget, Jean (1966) *The Psychology of Intelligence.* Totowa, New Jersey: Littlefield Adams & Co.

Piaget, Jean and Inhelder, Barbel (1969) *The Psychology of the Child.* New York: Basic Books.

Pick Jr., Herbert L. (1989) Motor Development: The Control of Action, *Developmental Psychology.* Vol. 25 (6), 867-870.

Shipley, Dale (1993) *Empowering Children, Play-Based Curriculum for Lifelong Learning.* Toronto, Canada: Nelson.

Simpson, Elizabeth J. (1972) in *The Psychomotor Domain.* Washington, D.C.: Gyrophon House. Published for National Special Media Institutes.

In this chapter you will learn about:

- Perceptual motor development
- Kinaesthesis
- Visual,auditory,tactile perception
- Body, spatial, directional,temporal awareness
- Learning opportunities

PERCEPTUAL MOTOR DEVELOPMENT

.....a harmony between mind and body, with the mind trained to use the body properly, and the body trained to respond to the expressive powers of the mind.

Howard Gardner

PERCEPTION

Perception is a process that interprets information obtained through the senses. It is the ability to recognize and take in stimuli, and store the unique interpretation of them for future recall. It is the senses that provide us with information about the world around us. This information is then processed by each individual based on unique internal schema, previous experience, and present stage of development. Children differ not only in the amount of perceptual information they have but in the way in which they interpret incoming stimuli(Piaget, 1966; Halverson, 1984). According to Allen and Marotz (1989), as a child matures, the ability to use information taken in through the senses increases in complexity.

Perception is a key component of motor learning (Williams, 1983, Holding, 1989, Halverson, 1977). Without perceptual development and a *feedback* system to interpret sensory data, motor development may be slowed. The term feedback will be used throughout to describe sensory information from external and internal sources. The way an object feels, the noise we hear in a room, or the smells around us all provide examples of external stimuli. Internal stimuli are messages we receive that come from inside our bodies, such as information about where a body part is located in relation to another body part, or information about whether our arms are crossed or not. Sensory information is raw data received by our brain via our sense organs.

Interpretation of data is based on perception. Previous experience provides the basis for interpretation of a situation and each new experience provides a new perspective. To promote positive motor development in young children, it is essential that you provide a variety of stimuli and stimulating situations for exploration as well as for guided discovery. Exploration involves independent investigation by the child, whereas guided discovery consists of verbal prompting by the adult or educator.

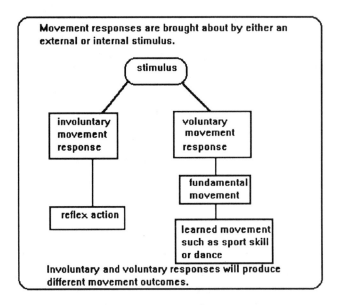

FIGURE 2.1. Movement responses as a result of a stimulus

Many movement responses change with an individual's natural development; however we cannot ignore the fact that there are also reactions to either external or internal stimuli. A stimulus essentially provides the impetus for a response. The stimulus acts as a catalyst for a reaction. Some reactions to a stimulus are involuntary while others are voluntary. *What is the difference?* Initially, motor abilities are a reflex or involuntary action (Allen and Marotz, 1989). Involuntary responses or reflexes are not consciously controlled, while voluntary responses are controlled actions. Voluntary movement responses begin as *fundamental* movements that begin without training.(Harrow, 1972). The initial fundamental movements are rudimentary in nature and include such abilities as rolling over, lifting the upper body, or creeping. These rudiments of movement form the basis for more advanced fundamental movements, which in turn form the basis for all later specialized motor or sports skills. Depending on the developmental stage, there may be a predominance of involuntary or voluntary responses, each one providing a different motor outcome. A stimulus can evoke an involuntary response such as the knee jerk caused by tapping on the top of the patellar region or it can lead to a voluntary response such as a child deciding to hang from a climbing frame, simply because it is there. Figure 2.1. on the preceding page, illustrates this stimulus-response relationship.

INTERPRETING PERCEPTUAL CUES

Perceptual motor development requires monitoring and interpreting information or sensory data, and responding to this data through movement. It refers to the movement interpretation an individual places on the information received through the senses. This motor response provides opportunity for learning through movement. Figure 2.2. illustrates how information received by the senses acts as a stimulus that provokes a spontaneous or learned movement.

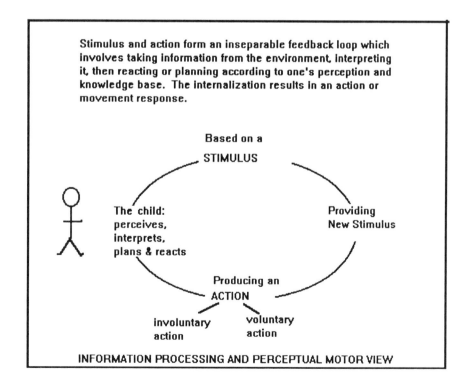

FIGURE 2.2. Perception of stimulus plays an active role in motor outcome

Initial stimulus is received by the individual, processed, and is reacted upon. This processing and reaction acts as feedback and reappears in the form of a new stimulus.

Five senses provide information through the external environment. They are smell, taste, touch, hearing, and sight. Of these, three seem to have a more obvious impact on movement than do the others. They are:

1. sight which leads to **visual perception**
2. hearing which leads to **auditory perception**
3. touch which leads to **tactile perception**

Perception in each of these sensory areas refers to the interpretation of the stimulus that enters the individual through the specified receptors (Harrow, 1972). Sensory information is taken in from the external environment and interpreted in the cognitive domain. The way information is processed varies with each child and more so in a child who has a visual or auditory impairment. When this happens, movement opportunities require adaptations via augmentation of other senses. We have provided a few adaptations throughout the text, but you will need to evaluate and make the changes that best suit your particular situation. We also offer some opportunities that you can try in order to sensitize yourself to the difficulties an individual goes through when they lack the input from any one sense.

Other perceptual information necessary for perceptual motor development is acquired through the internalization of perceptual elements. In her taxonomy on the psychomotor domain, Harrow (1972) classifies all internal perceptual elements under the term **kinaesthesis**. We see this as an oversimplification and for this reason have chosen to break down the internal elements into four distinct headings outlined below. Firstly, the reader will need to know that where internal perceptual elements are concerned there is a greater emphasis on stored information and feedback, rather than input. Secondly, the definition of the term kinaesthesis has evolved in recent years. It refers to movements and static limb positions that are related to information taken in by the sensory receptors. These receptors can be muscles, joints, tendons, skin, auditory, and/or vestibular apparatus(Holding, 1989). Static limb position refers to holding a part of the body still.

The four internal perceptual elements individuals use to find our more about their bodies are:

1. **body awareness**
2. **spatial awareness**
3. **directional awareness**
4. **temporal awareness**

As we have already noted, perceptual abilities change with maturation and experience. Furthermore, children and adults extract information from the environment differently. As the infant matures, there is a greater ability to differentiate the stimuli, moving from a sensorimotor phase of development to one where abstract information can be used. For example, a simple game of Sally Says is not possible for very young children to carry out successfully. By the time they process the information about where the body part being named is, and by the time they figure out how to move it, an older child will have long completed the task. Younger children take much longer to differentiate the stimuli while older children respond almost automatically.

Young children usually require a great deal of information before they are able to perceptually interpret an event. As they mature to adulthood, they become more able to recognize events without complete information. They can piece together a "whole" relying on past information, memory, and their perceptual skills.

Perceptual and sensory information are necessary in order for the "movers to know their bodies and know their movements" (Keogh & Sugden, 1985, p. 265). Children must develop an understanding of their bodies. For example, in a child's first game of hide and seek, she may hide her upper body and feel perfectly out of view. She has a notion that since she cannot see you, you cannot see her. The young child, still egocentric, understands her perception to be reality, and therefore assumes that everyone else's perception is the same as hers is. Research shows (Cherry, et al.; 1989, Schirrmacher, 1988) that different types of information are processed by different hemispheres of the brain. There are two hemispheres referred to as the left and right. The left hemisphere tends towards thinking abilities, logic, reasoning, and linear thought. The right hemisphere is known for intuitive, non-verbal, visual, and holistic thought. The functions of each hemisphere are equally important but it is the dominant one that tends to process information first (Meiste Vitale, 1985). This is important to the educator as it infers that children may respond differently to the same piece of equipment or activity set up. The right brain dominant individual may approach a room full of large equipment eagerly and quickly, seemingly trying out everything at once, while the left brain thinker might spend time carefully examining one piece of equipment at length.

As learning occurs, there is an increased capacity to select, plan, execute, and then evaluate one's own movements. Learning occurs in both hemispheres of the brain and in more than one domain at a time. Learning opportunities provided may focus on one particular perceptual area but it is unlikely they will be limited to only that one. Usually there are secondary perceptual areas that are developed simultaneously. Kinaesthetic awareness can be successfully developed through many types of learning opportunities and is strongly evidenced in creative movement, a topic we felt merited a chapter of its own, Chapter 11.

We will begin our discussion of the sensorimotor processes with the external senses, how they take in information, and how they impact motor development. This is followed by a discussion of the internal perceptual elements that affect movement and learning.

Visual Perception

What is visual perception? It is a combination of the physical ability to see as well as a process "that involve the pick up, transmission and interpretation of information by peripheral and central nervous system structures"(Williams, 1983, p.73). This means that you may pick up information through your eyes from something you see or look at. You might process information about such distinctions as the shade, colour, shape, or even location of an object. That information is then stored for future use. The ability to see is innate in the normal child, however "visual perception is in large part a learned phenomena"(Williams, 1983, p. 73). We can all see the markings on a paper that spell out someone's name. This does not mean that we have any cognitive understanding of what those markings mean. A triangle on its side in Western culture is just that, but to the Inuit it represents the letter "A" and has meaning attached to it. The perception of the visualized symbol is a learned phenomena. Another example relates to a piece of equipment that a child is trying to adjust her body to. In trying to go around a slide in the park, the child must see it and judge its width and girth before going around it. The visual perception yields a spatial orientation and provides a "cognitive mapping of the environment"(Gibson, p.163).

At about six months of age children work to integrate visual and movement capabilities. The child's visual-motor impressions begin with manipulations of her own body. As the visual-motor impressions of the world around develop, the infant begins to manipulate objects. This can be observed as she reaches out to grasp an object.

In general, you should provide many opportunities for an infant to explore the same object so that visual perceptions and an internal schema can be formed. A variety of toys of different shapes, sizes, and colours should be made available for exploration. You can also hold objects at varying distances and encourage the child to look at them. Try holding a bright object in front of the infant at her eye level. Move it slowly from one side of the body to the other. Repeat this until the infant no longer shows interest in the following the object with her eyes. At this point let the infant hold the object in her hand and explore it using the sense of touch.

Still more advanced is the interception of a moving object. This requires the added visual skill of **tracking**. Tracking is the ability to follow a moving object. It is an important skill used in **eye-hand** coordination, **eye-foot** coordination, and reading. Once visual tracking is in place, the child can begin to intercept a moving object. This is a more advanced skill that requires a combination of perceptual skills: the use of visual tracking, timing (temporal awareness), and reaching (spatial awareness).

It is important to note that visual acuteness and perceptual coordination of the infant may not be at the same developmental level. Think for example of the toddler who reaches for a spoon to self-feed, carefully brings the spoon to her mouth, and misses. The child will learn this task through practise and maturation. Perceptual skills and manipulative skills must each reach a certain level for the child to achieve motor success.

By about age two, many well learned actions are followed with less visual attention. For example, a child learning to walk will pay close attention to the foot path and to each foot, much like an adult staring at her feet as she learns to dance. Proficiency develops and the individual no longer relies on visual cues for motor success. Cues become internalized and messages are interpreted through kinaesthesis.

To get a sense of the importance of visual awareness, try the following exercise. Either find a friend to try this with, or if you are in a group, divide the group in pairs. One partner is blindfolded while the other acts as a guide. The blindfolded person holds on to the guide's arm for support. The blindfolded person tries to walk around the room or down a corridor. After five minutes of exploration, reverse roles. Ask yourself the following questions: *What other senses did I rely on most to compensate for the lack of vision? How did it feel to grope around the room? How did being blindfolded effect my speed of travel?*

Auditory Perception

Auditory perception is the ability to hear different sounds and to distinguish one from another. Listening, the ability to remember sounds, and sound patterns form a part of auditory perception. Listening skills (and therefore auditory perception) can be improved by providing appropriate activities. Listening is an important skill that can be enhanced early in a child's life. This skill can easily lead to success in many other areas of one's life. We do not advocate long, boring listening sessions. Rather, provide opportunities to heighten auditory discrimination so that children know what to listen for.

According to Meiste Vitale (1985) auditory listening is processed differently by right-handed and left-handed people. The left hemisphere of the brain controls auditory listening in people who have a right-handed dominance. In left-handed individuals it is usually the right hemisphere that controls auditory listening. Some of us, it appears, learn better through the auditory sense, while others seem to learn better through visual cues. Educators can use this knowledge by providing experiences that will integrate both right and left hemisphere. For further study about right and left brain dominance we refer you to Claire Cherry (1988) or Meiste Vitale (1985) to mention a few.

Auditory awareness is one of the perceptual elements involved in music, music appreciation, and general attention to sound. Both singing and listening to music will add an important dimension to the psychomotor curriculum. Music provides opportunities for rhythm and rhythmic expression. By providing musical instruments coupled with props such as scarves during free play, you can stimulate creative movement. There are songs that can be used for finger plays, music for creative dance, instruments for creative expression, and taped music played in the background during free play. The choice of music can affect the mood in the class. For example, slow, quiet music will provide a calming atmosphere in the room while upbeat lively music will encourage a higher level of activity and excite a group. It is up to you to determine what impact you wish the music to have on the children.

Infants are able to hear sounds and determine their source. An easy activity to promote auditory development in younger children is to provide noisy toys. At an early age, children are also able to distinguish one person's voice from another. Children can respond to verbal instructions once language understanding is in place. They also enjoy listening to the vocal sounds they produce, accidentally at first, then deliberately. Children have great fun mimicking adult sounds. Movement responses to sounds and specific rhythms are not uncommon, as exemplified in the following **spontaneous play** anecdote:

◆ ◆ ◆

> *A song from Snow White was on in the background. Every time the marching tune came on in "Hi ho hi ho, It's off to work we go," they all got up from their play, as if on cue, and marched around the room. They would then return to their play as if uninterrupted.*

◆ ◆

This action initiated by the children demonstrates a child's strong sense of rhythm. It also shows us how background music provides a supplementary component to the curriculum. Children listen to sounds and music in the environment without conscious awareness.

Tactile Awareness

Tactile awareness involves the sense of touch through receptors in the skin. Through the sense of touch we can distinguish between soft and hard, smooth and rough, as well as hot and cold. Those of us who learn best by doing may be tactile learners. That is, we take in information best through the sense of touch in our hands and other body parts. Tactile learners need to physically experience a task in order to learn it best. This infers that information may be processed first through the right hemisphere. Some young children may need to touch in order to understand a concept. They may need to hold a triangle, for example, and feel the edges and angles in order to assign cognitive meaning to the word triangle. Others might understand the concept of the shape simply by seeing it drawn on a two-dimensional surface.

Water and sand play provide tactile experiences by way of feeling the texture of both materials. Sand sifts slowly through the fingers and has a grainy feel, while water slips between the fingers quickly feeling wet and light in weight. You should find it easy to provide many opportunities which foster tactile experiences. Free play materials can be set out to provide exploration of various textures. Collage materials for art provide exciting textures. Use feathers, glue, sand, buttons, or just about anything you can think of.

To provide small motor, tactual experiences, you can set out play dough, clay, finger painting, or soap painting - to mention a few. In presenting large motor opportunities you can set out a variety of balls such as nerf balls, coosh balls, bouncy rubber balls, and many others. Other textured objects such as bean bags and scarves can be introduced as a part of the psychomotor program.

As have others (Beaty, 1992), we have used woodworking with children as young as four years old and found it provides excellent opportunity for tactile exploration. Participants use both fine and gross motor movements. They hammer in nails, sand the wood, lift, carry, and generally manipulate the materials.

Body Awareness

Through body awareness the child develops a sense of self. A person's sense of self or the way she feels about herself is often linked to the awareness she has of her body. A child who has a positive perception about her physical self will tend to have a positive self-image. Body awareness includes knowledge of where the body parts are, what they are called, how the different parts of the body work, as well as the recognition that the body is a separate entity from the rest of the world. One of the first milestones an infant goes through is the knowledge that her body is separate from the world around her. This was first noted by Piaget(1966) in his study of the sensorimotor phase of development.

First, there is a hierarchy of knowledge or understanding of body awareness. Children acquire knowledge of where their body parts are located, then they become capable of naming the different parts of their body. They develop an awareness of how each body part functions and an understanding of the relationship between different body parts. Once an understanding of function and relationship of body parts is achieved, children can be given tasks related to contracting and relaxing specific muscles. We have done this successfully with children ranging from four to twelve years of age. Children of four and five have greater ease relaxing specific muscles than contracting them. It appears that contracting the muscles requires greater concentration.

Body awareness has a far greater scope than just the physical knowledge and understanding of how the parts of the body function. It also includes the perception that an individual has about her exterior self. The development of the child's coordination plays an important role in the development of her body image. Spontaneous play provides opportunities for children to develop positive body image. For example, running outdoors just for the sake of running is one such opportunity. Another involves the child who is exploring a climbing frame for the tenth time and is still finding new ways to use her body. Each successful climbing attempt brings the child a greater degree of self-confidence about what her body is capable of doing. Two wonderful games that encourage awareness of body parts and how they function include the Human Machine and Twister. See Learning Opportunity numbers 15 and 19.

Photo 2.1. Preschool children enjoy a game of Back to Back.

Spatial Awareness

Spatial awareness involves an understanding of the space around us. Our bodies take up space and we are surrounded by space. How do our bodies fit through objects, how much space does an object take, how far are we from an object? All these involve concepts of near and far, over and under, through and around, high and low. The perceptual ability to distinguish the distance an object is from oneself is a combination of developmental process and learned skill, usually assisted by visual cues.

The interdependence of all domains on children's learning is especially obvious in the development of spatial awareness. Vision plays an important role. Usually one sees an object before assessing its location, its shape, or size. Those who are visually impaired will need to rely greatly on the kinaesthetic sense or on auditory perception to assist in determining where their body is in relation to objects around.

The space around us includes personal, indoor, and outdoor space. Personal space is the space immediately around us. General space includes both indoor and outdoor space bounded by the environment we are in. Indoor space can be manipulated by the educator to provide a variety of challenging exploratory situations. Changing the placement of furniture, for example, will affect the pathways of the classroom, the noise level, the way in which children transport objects such as blocks and wheeled vehicles, and general movemeny within the classroom. Pathways are the patterns on the floor used in moving about. As we get older we tend to become rigid in our thinking around the use of space. Ask a group of adults to move to some specified beat anywhere in a large open space. The tendency will be to move in a circle with all participants going in the same direction. In our section on creative movement we will suggest some ideas to expand horizons and open up movement pathways as well as help develop an understanding of the space around us.

The outdoor environment can provide large open spaces to run in or smaller spaces such as a sand play area for digging and sand building. These opportunities will provide valuable information needed for daily existence that will assist in the development of spatial awareness.

Directional Awareness

Directional awareness encompasses a number of concepts. It refers to an understanding that there are two sides to the body as well as a front and a back. Directional Awareness includes moving the body up and down, forward and backward, and from side to side, as well as an understanding of laterality. Laterality is an underlying concept that must be achieved for successful development of directional awareness. "If a child develops laterality, it implies that he can move corresponding parts of the body separately, together, simultaneously or in a cross lateral pattern" (Pangrazi & Dauer, 1972). It is an internal understanding of sidedness. The knowledge that there are two sides to the body, and an external ability to move the body in certain ways is part of the development of laterality. People ultimately show preference for one side of their body over the other. The "simple knowledge of sidedness is a perceptual distinction, whereas attachment of right or left labels is more a cognitive distinction" (Keogh and Sugden, 1985, p. 277). Prior to age six we should not expect or require that children have cognitive knowledge of right and left. They should have a knowledge of sidedness and concepts such as two eyes, two hands, etc. In the preschool years, movement activities should provide opportunities for children to move their whole body and parts of their bodies in a variety of combinations. These experiences should include moving in different directions, such as forward and backward, but should not insist on any cognitive labels of left and right. You can help develop an understanding of direction by using verbal reinforcement when playing with the children. For example, such cues as,

"Ali, that is an interesting way to go through the tunnel," or "I see you went over the hoop with a large step" will assist in making the link between a movement and its cognitive meaning.

Directional awareness is an important element in the development of reading skills as it involves the distinction between lower case letters of "b" and "d," which are commonly reversed in the young child's mind. Reading is a skill that can move from right to left as in English or French, or left to right as in Hebrew or Arabic. The important commonality is that each language has a consistent directional reading pattern.

Temporal Awareness

Temporal awareness has come to mean many things that involve a multi-dimensional perspective. It has far reaching impact in daily life and has relevance to movement activities in many ways, such as sequencing, reaction time, concepts of fast and slow, rhythm and tempo. It is also an abstract concept that involves an internal awareness of a time structure. For example look at your watch to see what time it is, then close your eyes for five minutes. When you think that five minutes has passed open your eyes to see what time has really passed. *What does this tell you about your internal awareness of time?*

Initially there is a recognition and awareness of before and after. Later comes an understanding of sequence or order in carrying out actions. Perceptual elements needed for sequencing, ordering of events, the understanding of before and after, all lie within logical mathematical intelligence(Gardner, 1993) or the cognitive domain. The notion of time-keeping or of the understanding of concepts such as minute, hour, week, etc. is a cognitive skill as well. It does not appear to play an important role in motor development but is very much a part of team sports as the child needs to pace herself during a game. Another important dimension of temporal awareness includes **reaction time**. This includes the way in which an individual adjusts her body to react to an incoming object. Depending on the position or the speed of an object, such as a ball, the individual will process information and move her body to successfully intercept the moving ball. Timing also refers to adjusting the speed of one's movements in order to fulfil certain higher level motor functions. For example, an individual adjusts the speed of a run before an aerial move in gymnastics in order to achieve the necessary momentum.

Slow and fast, sustained actions or quick movements, as well as experiences involving the rhythm, tempo, or beat of music are important components of temporal awareness. They can include reaction to an external rhythm or beat as in music, especially percussion instruments.

Many free play opportunities can be designed to encourage cognitive development in this area. Puzzles involving sequence will not only develop fine motor manipulation, but they will also begin to introduce the abstract idea of ordering of events. Through hands-on manipulative experiences, children can explore the notion of what comes first and what comes second. In the daycare or nursery, there is a schedule. It is important to maintain this schedule, although it is not necessary to adhere to the specific hour.

♦ ♦ ♦

> *Cinzia a recent early childhood graduate, was quite excited when the first snow fall arrived. She decided to take the children outside first thing in the morning (rather than before lunch which was usually the case) so that they might enjoy the snowfall. Cinzia and the children spent close to an hour outside frolicking in the snow. They went back into the daycare around 10:30. As soon as the children were undressed they all began to sit at the table. When Cinzia told them that they could go play they all wanted to know where their lunch was!*

♦ ♦

Predictability assists children in understanding the notion of sequence or order of events. When there is a change in the schedule discussion needs to occur. It is worthy of note that some studies have shown children who are left hemisphere dominant seem to have a good sense of time. Children who are right hemisphere dominant, on the other hand, seem to have a poor sense of time (Meiste Vitale; 1985 Cherry, 1989).

CHAPTER HIGHLIGHTS

Perceptual motor development is defined as a movement response to a stimulus. When this movement response is involuntary it is referred to as a reflex, when it is voluntary it is a controlled movement. Within voluntary responses are fundamental movement skills as well as the more refined combination skills needed for many sports.

It is a combination of perception, the unique way in which an individual sees the world and performs operations, and hands on experience, that yields the greatest learning. "Perceptual activities develop with age both in number and in quality"(Piaget & Inhelder, 1969, p.35).

In conclusion, as children develop and take in information there is an unfolding of potential. It is worth noting that perceptual motor skills form the foundation for many academic and life skills that children will encounter.

The following learning opportunities have a "focus" as an indicator of the primary perceptual components involved. Ratios throughout will represent adult to child.

LEARNING OPPORTUNITIES

1. ‖ <u>Feel that Beat</u>

   Age: six to ten months

   Ratio: one to one

   Procedure:

   Introduce some rhythmic music. While holding the child, move to the beat of the music. Vary the tempo and beat of the music. Select music from a variety of cultures as each one has a unique rhythmic quality and flavour.

   focus: auditory perception, temporal awareness

2. ‖ <u>Head and Shoulders</u>

   Age: six months to five years

   Ratio: Will vary depending on the variation.

   Procedure:

   The following verse is chanted:

   > Head and shoulders, knees and toes.
   > Knees and toes, knees and toes, knees and toes.
   > Head and shoulders, knees and toes.
   > Eyes, ears, mouth, and nose.

   Infants and toddlers: adult points to the body parts as she names them.
   Two to five: children point to their own body parts.
   Five and up: children work in pairs and point to their friends' body parts as they are called out.

Variation: Sing it backwards.

Variation: Ages three and up carry out physical actions instead of just pointing to the various body parts. On <u>head</u>, shake your head, on <u>shoulders</u>, lift your shoulders up and down, on <u>knees</u>, bend your knees, on <u>toes</u>, go up on your toes.

focus: body awareness, auditory perception, directional awareness

3. ‖ <u>Feely Box</u>

    Age: eighteen months to five years

    Ratio: eighteen months, one to three
                  three to five years, one to twelve

    Procedure:

For eighteen months to three years old. Show the children three to five objects that you plan to place in the feely box. Pass the box around the circle. Each child has a turn to put her hand in to try and describe the object she is touching. Her descriptions continue until someone guesses what the object is. She then pulls the object out of the box to show everyone. The game continues. See glossary for a description of a feely box.

For ages three to five. Increase the number of objects placed in the box. Objects are not shown to the children before hand.

focus: tactile perception, auditory perception

4. ‖ <u>Ball Roll</u>

    Age: eighteen months

    Ratio: one to one

    Procedure:

Sit on the floor facing the child. You are both seated with your legs open in a "V" position. A large rubber ball, approximately 8"(20 centimeters) to 10" (25 centimeters) in diameter is rolled from you to the child. Encourage her to follow the ball with her eyes as it moves toward her. Have her roll the ball back. Repeat the activity as long as she is still having fun and seems interested.

focus: visual perception, spatial awareness, directional awareness

5. ‖   Spaghetti Arms

Age: two and up

Ratio: two to five years, one to five
five and up, one to twelve

Procedure:

Ask children to lie flat on their backs, and close their eyes if they feel comfortable to do so. Encourage them to relax and make their arms soooo loose, so that when you come around and try to lift their arms to shake them, they will wobble like cooked spaghetti. Children aged five and up like to help shake up the spaghetti arms.

focus: body awareness, auditory awareness, tactile perception

6. ‖   Objects

Age: two and a half and up

Ratio: two and a half to four years, one to six
four years and up, one to ten

Procedure:

Select three objects that will be of interest to the children, each with a different textures. For example, a pine cone is hard and pointy, a bean bag is soft, smooth, and lumpy. Pass the object around the circle singing the following chant:

"Round and round the object goes and where it stops, nobody knows."

The child who is holding the object at the end of the chant tries to select one word that describes how the object feels. Repeat the chant while passing the object around again. After the second child gives a new description to the object, repeat both the first and second child's descriptive word before passing the object around again. Introduce the next object when you feel the timing is right.

focus: tactile perception, directional awareness, auditory perception

7. ‖   <u>Hokey Pokey</u>

   Age: two a half and up

   Ratio: two and a half to five years, one to five
                   five years and up, one to twelve

Procedure:

We have modified the original song to enhance knowledge of sidedness and body awareness instead of placing emphasis on left and right. We suggest you begin by selecting large body parts and eventually introducing smaller and funnier body parts to take this experience from simple to complex. The words we provide are but one possible adaptation.

>   You put your stomach in
>   You take you stomach out
>   You put your stomach in
>   And you shake it all about.
>
>   You put your bum in
>   You take your bum out
>   You put your bum in
>   And you shake it all about.
>   Etc...

focus: directional awareness, body awareness, auditory perception

8. ‖   <u>Who Lives There?</u>

   Age: three and up

   Ratio: three years, one to seven
                   five years, one to twelve

Procedure:

In a cloth shoe bag place an object that is familiar to the children. We recommend such items as balloons blown up, a small ball, a set of keys, or a block. Sit in a circle with your group of children. Pass the bag around and let the children feel the outside of it without seeing what is inside. Let them try and guess what is inside. With large groups of children we recommend passing two bags around, each with the same object in it.

focus: tactile perception

9. ‖ Magic Tambourine

Age:　　three to 8 years

Ratio:　　one to eight

Procedure:

Using a tambourine or drum, create a beat and encourage the children to stomp and walk around the room. Play a strong beat for stomping and a softer, slower beat for tiptoeing. Encourage children to listen to the different sound qualities. Together with the children, agree on a "stopping" sound and a "going" sound. This will be useful later in implementing creative movement.

focus: auditory perception, directional awareness

10. ‖ Stiff as a Board

Age:　　three and up

Ratio:　　one to seven

Procedure:

This is the same setup as Spaghetti Arms, but the children are asked to tighten their muscles so much that when you try to lift them, they will not bend their bodies, not even at the waist. You then try to lift each child by placing one arm under each shoulder and lift them slowly to a standing position.

note: Because this exercise requires lifting, we suggest you try it only if you feel your back is strong enough. Remember to bend your knees before lifting.

focus: body awareness

11. ‖   <u>Sally Says</u>

Age: three years and up

Ratio: one to eight

Procedure:

In this game, like in "Simon Says," a caller verbalizes an action and the participants carry out the action. In our version of this game, there is no elimination. When a child misses the cue, she simply continues the game sitting down. If she misses when she is sitting, then she continues to play, standing up. Cues to enhance body awareness are perfect, such as "touch your head, or wiggle your toes." (Another variation of this learning opportunity is provided in Chapter nine, Opportunity 12.)

focus: body awareness, directional awareness, auditory perception

12. ‖   <u>Little Peter Rabbit</u>

Ages: three to six years

Ratio: one to eight

Procedure:

Seat the children in a circle on the floor. Introduce the song Little Peter Rabbit:

>   Little Peter Rabbit had a fly upon his _____
>   Little Peter Rabbit had a fly upon his _____
>   Little Peter Rabbit had a fly upon his _____
>   And he flicked it, till it flew away!

Before starting the song, give each child a sticker. Ask one child where she would like to put her sticker. Then encourage each child to put the sticker on that part of the body. You then begin the song and fill in the blank with the part of the body.

>   Little Peter Rabbit had a fly upon his <u>ear.</u> (etc).

The song continues until everyone has had a turn to name a part of the body. Each time a different body part is named the sticker is moved around. Finally, you ask the children to hide their "fly" in a special place till next time.

focus: body awareness, auditory perception, visual perception

13. ‖   Balance Board

    Age: three years and up

    Ratio: open activity

    Procedure:

Set up a balance beam (the height will vary depending on the age and ability of the children) or balance board. Encourage children to explore by instructing them to go across, over, forwards, backwards, and around. In this way the child must determine the best foot pattern and must find the best point of balance. Through movement, the children are taught language concepts of over, around, and across.

focus: directional awareness, body awareness, visual perception

14. ‖   Kick Time

    Age: three and a half years and up

    Ratio: open activity

    Procedure:

Provide a stationary ball. Ask the child to kick the ball so that it rolls quickly. Then ask her to kick it so that it rolls slowly. Problem solving and perceptual understanding is developed and increased by asking her, "What did you do to make the ball move slowly? How did you make it move quickly?"

focus: temporal awareness, visual awareness, directional awareness

15. ‖ Twister(Milton Bradley)

    Age: four and up

    Ratio: one to five

Procedure:

This game can be purchased commercially or can be modified and constructed by the educator. The basic principle is to provide a large rectangular sheet of plastic or cloth about 4 feet by 5 feet(12 meters by 15 meters), placed on the floor. On this sheet, the educator designs four rows of five or six coloured circles, or alternating shapes.

A spinner with matching shapes or colours is used to determine which space the children will place a hand or foot on. If the educator calls "hand on red", the child playing must place one hand on a red shape. The next call may be "hand on yellow". This would mean that she would place her other hand on the yellow. The game continues until the children hands and feet are all tangled together.

Twister is best played without shoes. It is great fun both indoors and outdoors.

focus: body awareness,directional awareness, spatial awareness

16. ‖ Person to Person

    Age: five and up

    Ratio: partner activity

Procedure:

In this activity children are connecting different body parts. For example, if you call out "knee to elbow," one child must find another in the class and they must attach themselves together by the knee of one child and the elbow of the other. The next instruction may be "heel to finger." The children each need to find another person to attach themselves to using the new body parts that have been called out. As children become proficient at this game silly combinations, such as "knee to nose," can be introduced.

focus: body awareness, directional awareness, spatial awareness

17. ‖ ZigZag

> **Age:**   five years
>
> **Ratio:**   one to twelve
>
> **Procedure:**

Play classical music. Instruct the children to move in zigzags anywhere in the room until the music stops. The music is resumed and the children are instructed to move in another suggested pattern, such as a square.

focus: directional awareness, auditory perception

18. ‖ Back to Back

> **Age**:   six and up
>
> **Ratio:**   partner activity
>
> **Procedure:**

Two children sit on the floor, back to back. They interlock arms and try to stand up by pushing their body weight against each other.

focus: body awareness

19. ‖ Human Machine

> **Age:**   six and up
>
> **Ratio:**   one to twelve
>
> **Procedure:**

Ask one child to go to the middle of an open area and ask her to move one body part repetitively. For example, she may stand up and move her arm up and down. A second child is then asked to attach herself to the first child in any way she chooses to and she in turn moves one body part.(It does not have to be the same body part.) The second child may, for example, decide to sit on the floor, hold on to the first child's leg, and bob his head up and down. A third child is then asked to connect to the machine. This is continued until all the children are connected and moving their body parts.

focus: body awareness, directional awareness

20. ‖   <u>Sound Walk</u>

Age: all

Ratio: will vary depending on the age of the children

Procedure:

Go with the children for a walk outdoors. This provides exercise, fresh air, and opportunity to take notice of the many wonderful sounds. Point out the sounds of birds, cars, snow crunching under your feet in winter, or rustling leaves on trees above. This will heighten the child's sensitivity and awareness to sound.

focus: auditory perception, visual perception

REFERENCES

Allen, Eileen K. and Marotz, Lynn (1989) *Developmental Profiles, From Birth to Six.* Albany, New York: Delmar Publishers.

Bailey, Rebecca Anne & Burton, Elsie Carter (1982) *The Dynamic Self.* St. Louis, Missouri: The C.V. Mosby Company.

Beaty, Janice (1992) *Skills for Preschool Teachers.* Fourth edition, Don Mills, Ontario: MacMillan Publishing.

Cherry, Claire, Godwin, Douglas, Staples, Jesse (1989) *Is The Left Brain Always Right?* Belmont, California: Fearon Teacher Aids.

Cratty, Bryant J. (1986) *Perceptual and Motor Development in Infants and Children.* New Jersey: Prentice-Hall.

Fineman, Mark (1981) *The Inquisitive Eye.* New York: Oxford University Press.

Gallahue, David L. (1982) *Developmental Movement Experiences for Children.* New York: John Wiley.

Gardner, Howard (1993) *Multiple Intelligences, The Theory in Practise.* New York: Basic Books.

Gibson, J.J. (1966) *The Senses Considered as Perceptual Systems.* Boston: Houghton Mifflin Company.

Halverson, Lolas E. & Robertson, Mary Ann (1977) *Physical Education for Children: A Focus on the Teaching Process.* Philadelphia: Lea & Febiger.

Halverson, Lolas E.& Robertson, Mary Ann (1984) *Developing Children - Their Changing Movement.* Philadelphia: Lea & Febiger.

Harrow, Anita J. (1972) *A Taxonomy of the Psychomotor Domain.* New York: David McKay Company.

Holding, Dennis H. (1989) *Human Skills.* New York: John Wiley and Sons.

Keogh, Jack and Sugden, David (1985) *Movement Skill Development.* New York: MacMillan Publishing Company.

Meiste Vitale, Barbara (1985) *Unicorns Are Real, A Right-Brained Approach to Learning.* Rolling Hills Estates, California: Jalmar Press.

Morison, Ruth (1969) *A Movement Approach to Educational Gymnastics.* London, England: Aldin Press.

Pangrazi, Robert P. & Dauer, Victor P. (1972) *Movement in Early Childhood and Primary Education.* Minneapolis: Burgess Publishing Company.

Piaget, Jean (1966) *The Psychology of Intelligence* Totowa, New Jersey: Littlefield Adams Co.

Piaget, Jean and Inhelder, Barbel (1969) *The Psychology of the Child.* New York: Basic Books Inc.

Shipley, Dale (1993) *Empowering Children, Play-Based Curriculum for Lifelong Learning.* Toronto, Canada: Nelson.

Shirrmacher, Robert (1988) *Art and Creative Development For Young Children.* San Jose: City College, Delmar.

Willims, Harriet G. (1983) *Perceptual and Motor Development.* New Jersey: Prentice-Hall.

In this chapter you will learn about:

- Balance
    - base of support
    - static and dynamic balance
    - visual cues and balance
    - and the environment
- Physical fitness
    - cardiovascular endurance
    - muscular strength
    - muscular endurance
    - flexibility
    - fitness for life
- Learning opportunities

BALANCE AND PHYSICAL FITNESS

Every human being develops according to a highly individualized time clock, a biological schedule that helps determine the readiness for various fitness activities and sports, as well as the ability to participate in planning and executing a fitness program.

Dr. Kenneth Cooper

The focus of this chapter is on balance and physical fitness, two separate but related topics. Both are underlying principles of our motor skill development and are components necessary for the refinement of motor skills.

Our discussion will concentrate on the two types of balance: static and dynamic, and how they impact on the child's movement. The topic of physical fitness will concentrate on cardiovascular endurance, muscular strength, muscular endurance, and flexibility.

BALANCE

We all need balance, a fundamental requirement essential to the performance of all motor skills. Balance is a physical, psychological, and cognitive task. The child's "sense of balance or imbalance is a visual, auditory and kinaesthetic sensing of stability in his environment" (Gerhardt, 1973, p.19). Without it an infant would not sit or stand, a child would not walk or run, and an adult would find it very difficult to perform many day-to-day movement tasks. "Technically, balance is not a skill but a rather important movement quality underlying the performance of a large group of skills" (Cratty, 1986, p.188) and "there is little doubt that for the young child, balance is an integral part of the skilful acquisition and performance of many motor tasks" (Williams, 1983, p.26). All fundamental skills require successful mastery of this ability.

A good example of this mastery of balance is when children begin the process of standing and walking. They rely on either objects or people to give them support. In this beginning stage, children do not have the balance nor the strength to stand and/or walk on their own. You will often see children use a table to pull themselves into a standing position. Initially, they will hold onto the table and then gradually start to let go, first for short periods of time and then for longer and longer periods. At this time, if led by an adult, they are able to walk. However, without adult assistance their ability to walk is unsuccessful. In this situation, the children understand the concept of walking but their sense of balance is not yet adequately developed, inhibiting independent walking. In this chapter we limit our discussion of walking to issues related to balance. The actual mechanics of walking are discussed in Chapter 5.

If we were unable to maintain our balance we would be in disequilibrium. Think of two children playing on a seesaw in the park. *What happens when one child is heavier than the other?* The weight is not evenly distributed and the two children become unbalanced. They have difficulty manoeuvring the seesaw in the way in which it was designed to move. Think of your body in somewhat the same way. Imagine if your weight was not evenly distributed. *Would you be able to move the way in which your body was designed to move?* According to Sanders(1992) we are on balance when our weight is evenly distributed on each side of our body.

Base of Support and Centre of Gravity

Kirchner (1992) explains balance as being able to keep our bodies in a stationary position and to resist the force of gravity while moving through our environment. Balance is achieved through a combination of muscular strength and the mastery of gravity. When we are balanced we find our centre of gravity to be over the **base of support** (Graham,Holt/Hale,Parker, 1993). Base of support refers to the parts of your body that come in contact with the surface or the ground, and the amount of surface you come in contact with while maintaining balance. Research (Kirchner, 1992; Adams, 1991; Graham 1993; et al;) indicates that as individuals we sometimes have an easier time balancing when we have a wide base of support versus a narrower one. A wider base of support lowers the centre of gravity, making it easier to maintain balance. In some instances the parts of the body that come in contact with the floor need to be spread out, effectively widening the base of support. For example, infants beginning to walk rely on a wide base of support to maintain their balance. They walk with their legs about shoulder width apart. With experience and training, legs come in closer together, thereby narrowing the base of support. Think in terms of trying to walk on a slippery terrain where the footing is uncertain. It is easier to maintain your balance with a wide base of support.

Two things affect the centre of gravity. Firstly, it changes depending on the pose and stance of the body (Adams, 1991) and secondly, the centre of gravity shifts as a child grows. Young children have a centre of gravity that is higher than that of older more developmentally mature children and adults. For children the centre of gravity is usually in the middle of their chest, whereas in adults the centre of gravity is closer to the belly button (Thelen, 1983). Young children have a higher centre of gravity in part because their legs are usually short with respect to the rest of their body. Visual cues help children maintain balance as well. Visual perception internalizes visual cues from the external environment about the body in relation to the space around it.

Photo 3.1. Nine year old child tries to find her centre of gravity.

Static and Dynamic Balance

Balance manifests itself in two ways, statically and dynamically.   Motor tasks require either static balance, dynamic balance, or some combination of both.   In all tasks requiring static balance, the body maintains one position or shape.   Dynamic balance occurs while a person is moving.   Dynamic means active or changing and that is what the body does in dynamic balance.   It involves the "smooth transition of the body's centre of gravity from one base of support to another"(Adams, 1991, p. 60).   It is this shift that is essential in preventing the body from falling down.

Examples of static balance are seen in the infant's ability to hold his head up, sit unassisted, or stand on one foot.   Many gymnastic skills, such as in a headstand or handstand, require sophisticated use of static balance.   Children's ability to demonstrate static balance will increase with age as their centre of gravity shifts.   It is for this reason that not all children should be expected to balance on one foot before the age of six.   This expectation would only lead to failure (Cratty, 1986).   Children must be developmentally able to adjust their centre of gravity and shift to one foot in order to succeed at this task (Kirchner, 1992; Adams, 1991).   In photo 3.2. below, a preshool child calls upon skills of dynamic and static balance.

Photo 3.2. A young child explores the joy of balance.

Dynamic balance is brought into action when the child goes from the sitting to the standing position and "has to accommodate to a new centre of gravity" (Gerhardt, 1973, p.20). Other examples of dynamic balance can be seen as the body shifts position in running, jumping, or climbing.

A child's mastery of balance is a combination of maturation, practice and experience. For the younger child mastering gravity to maintain dynamic balance is a formidable task. According to Sanders (1992, p.49) " a child who always falls down when throwing or catching a ball or who cannot maintain balance when landing after a jump will find it difficult to develop movement skills and may be unable to move safely through the environment." In the schoolage child, gravity is challenged when higherlevel sports that involve constantly shifting the centre of gravity (such as basketball, soccer, or tennis) are attempted. A good example of the shifting of the centre of gravity is found in the sport of gymnastics as it involves many changes in direction, axial movements, and turning on the axis of one body part on the uneven bars. Gymnasts walking across a balance beam are also challenged to maintain balance. So are figure skaters who learn to challenge themselves by balancing on the blades of their skates.

Figure 3.1. illustrates the two different balance opportunities that you should provide for. Simple activity suggestions are provided for a variety of developmental levels.

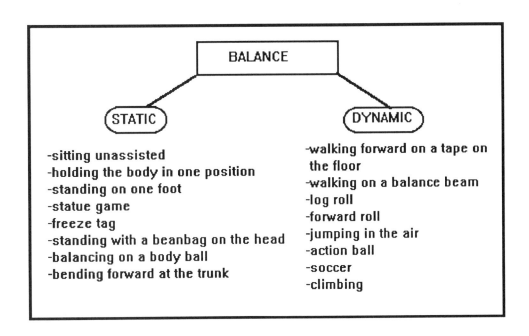

Figure 3.1. Some static and dynamic balance ideas

Visual Cues and Balance

Visual perception processes and responds to visual cues. Visually aided balance is evident in the spotting technique used by dancers. They need to focus on one object before beginning a pirouette. As the turn begins, they keep their eyes on a spot for as long as possible. This prevents dizziness by maintaining a stationary head position for as long as possible. When they can no longer see the spot, they quickly bring their head around and relocate the focal point as quickly as possible.

In the following picture of a child on a balance beam there are many factors that are called into play. The child must adapt to a narrow base of support. Visual cues will assist in stabilizing the body as the child uses a focal point to maintain stability.

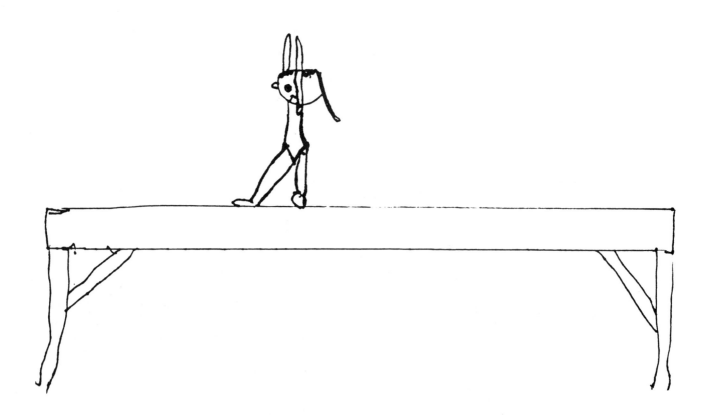

DRAWING 3.1. Balance beam perspective by seven year old child

Balance and the Environment

You can help children develop their balance by providing them with a variety of individual exploratory experiences as well as group games. Exploration tends to be more effective with younger preschoolers, while group games provide greater challenges for the older child.

Games such as Statue Game, Musical Freeze, Frozen Tag and the ideas offered in Figure 3.1. provide opportunities to practise both static and dynamic balance. Another effective way of developing dynamic and static balance is to have children place an object on different body parts. A beanbag can be placed on the head or foot. To develop static balance, children should then try to stand in one spot without dropping the beanbag. To develop dynamic balance encourage them to walk around with the beanbag in place without dropping it.

Equipment setup plays a pivotal role in the child's step by step mastery of balance. Table 3.1. provides a progression involving walking on a balance beam that we have found useful. These easy-to-follow steps encourage the dynamic balance required in learning to walk across a balance beam.

---

1. Put masking tape on the floor. Initially the tape should be placed in a straight line. Later, the tape can be placed in patterns such as squares, circles, or zigzags. Encourage the children to walk across the tape in any way they choose.

2. Set up a wide balance beam or plank of wood on the floor.

3. Set up a narrow balance beam on the floor.

4. Set up either a wide or narrow balance beam slightly elevated off the ground. Your choice will depend on the developmental level of the children you are working with.

5. The educator can invent challenges, such as placing beanbags along the tape on the floor for children to stop and pick up or as obstacles to walk over.

TABLE 3.1. Balance beam progression from simple to complex

PHYSICAL FITNESS

A tremendous amount of research, time and attention is presently being devoted to physical fitness, health-related physical fitness, and the physical well-being of children in both Canada and the United States. Traditionally, the subject of physical fitness has focused on the areas of cardiovascular endurance, muscular strength, muscular endurance, and flexibility. However in the early 1980s the scope of physical fitness was widened to include *body composition or body leanness.*

Fitness is not an activity but a necessary component of all movement. Being physically fit is important to all of us and a well designed movement program for children can be the key to their physical fitness for life. "Once acquired we do not remember fitness as we do motor skills, we must maintain it." (Lambert and Grube, 1988, p.71). Consequently physical fitness is not synonymous with physical education. Physical fitness is only one component or one aspect of any total physical education program.

"Health related physical fitness involves a level of physiological functioning that promotes good health and provides the resources for individuals to successfully perform their daily activities without undue fatigue" (Thomas et al. 1988, p.33). Physical fitness deals with those elements that determine how fit or how healthy our bodies are. Being physically fit is like having a well tuned car. Everyone knows that a car works better when it is fuelled, maintained, and run regularly, the body is no different. We all have a personal idea about what this means. Those of us who have had positive experiences in this area see physical fitness and sport as a lifelong pursuit. For all too many, negative experiences, modern day conveniences, and lack of opportunity have often led to the abandonment of physical fitness and the healthy way of life it fosters.

We can all think of the times we had to run around the football or soccer field at school once or twice a year in order to test how physically fit we were. Or, remember all those sit-ups and push-ups we just had to do! For many of us our memories of physical fitness were not fun. But they could have been and we want to advocate that you can and need to make physical fitness fun for the children. By the time numerous children finish Grade one they will already show signs of risk factors related to heart disease (Segal and Segal, 1992).

Fitness is the rage in video stores. It is on radio talk shows and almost every television channel has at least one half-hour fitness show. Articles for parents and educators are appearing in Parent's Magazine, Good Housekeeping, Homemaker's and National Geographic World. The Canadian government promotes physical fitness through Fitness Canada and Participation Canada. Western culture is obsessed with fitness. Yet the sad truth is that we are less physically fit today than we were ten years ago. (Segal and Segal, 1992; Roberts and Staver, 1992) *Why does this paradox exist?* According to Roberts and Staver (1992, p.70) "children's muscular strength and endurance are poor, while their percentage of body fat has increased over the past few years." This can be due to a combination of limited space availability for gross motor pursuits and high fat foods that are too readily available.

Often early childhood education facilities have a tendency to consider outdoor free play as the main provision for physical fitness. Elementary schools generally vary from province to province and state to state in the amount of time devoted weekly to being physically active. Although elementary schools often include at least some form of physical fitness session, it is all too often not enough or inadequately incorporated into the curriculum. This is especially true when we stop to think that grade school marks the beginning of a child's life behind his desk.

Questions you need to ask yourself include: *What constitutes a physically fit child? What skills should be practised to enhance fitness level? How can I develop fun and interesting opportunities for children that will increase their level of fitness?* The most important item that we need to stress is that a program of physical fitness for young children should not be a watered down version of what you experienced in your gym classes. It should be fun, active, focus on the health-related aspect of fitness, and provide opportunities that are developmentally appropriate. After all, can you really picture three-year-olds doing sit-ups all together?

Pangrazi and Dauer (1981, p. 19) advocate that movement programs should be organized in such a way that children "can develop a personalized level of fitness. For young children, this means sufficient gross motor activity on a regular basis to challenge growth." Since we believe that children are naturally movers and shakers, they will thrive in an environment that allows them to use their bodies.

Children need to be made aware of the importance of physical fitness. They need to be made aware of how vital it is to be physically fit and what the implications are of being physically fit. Your view of physical fitness can have a major impact on the way children will view it and your approach can help foster a positive lifelong attitude towards physical fitness. If you always stand on the sidelines and watch as children involve themselves in physical activity, their activity level will decrease. After all, most children will imitate the model you provide. So get involved and have fun!

We are often anxious to get children involved in organized sports as a way for them to become physically fit and maintain their physical fitness level. However, some children are encouraged to begin organized sports before they are developmentally ready. The unprepared child may have difficulty and become frustrated and discouraged and lose interest. Dr. Kenneth Cooper (1991) has found evidence indicating that by eight or nine children begin to decrease the amount of time they spend in those movement activities that would help them maintain their personal level of physical fitness.

We often think of the physically fit person as an athlete, but these two terms are not synonymous. A child can be physically fit but not have the developed motor skills or the interest to pursue athletic performance skills. Children increase their endurance, flexibility, and strength simply by being actively involved in some form of regular exercise (Roberts and Staver, 1992).

Our discussion of physical fitness will not include body composition or body leanness. We restrict our focus to the components of cardiovascular endurance, muscular endurance, muscular strength, and flexibility.

Cardiovascular Endurance

Cardiovascular endurance refers to the capacity of the heart and lung muscles to endure aerobic activity. Swimming, running, and biking are examples of aerobic activities. The heart rate is increased during the period of the activity. Cardiovascular endurance can be achieved by increasing the duration, frequency, and/or intensity of gross motor activity. Raising the intensity of activity increases the heart rate and the demand for oxygen. A school aged child can develop cardiovascular endurance through various sports activities. During a game of soccer, a child will run after a soccer ball and chase it down a field for an extended period of time. This fun experience raises the child's heart rate and promotes cardiovascular endurance.

Younger children instinctively love to run. There is often a tendency to restrict and limit children's desire to run, or we offer an area that is too small to promote vigorous activity. We may fear that the excitement will get out of hand, causing us to lose control of the group. This may result in an avoidance of vigorous play. We suggest that you give children the space they need and the opportunity to run.

The parachute is a great piece of apparatus that promotes cardiovascular endurance in children. A game of chase in the summer or crazy carpets in the winter are excellent ways to develop physical fitness in young children. Any vigorous open-ended activity sustained for at least ten minutes are beneficial.

A game of Duck Duck Goose appears to be fun for children but does not truly enhance the child's cardiovascular endurance. In this game the children are sitting in a circle and one child walks around the outside of the circle and touches the children on the head. Saying the word duck, duck duck... and at some point the child says goose to one child. This child then gets up and begins to chase the first child around the circle until the child gets back to the open spot. During this game the children spend much of their time sitting and waiting for their turn, not exercising their muscles. Generally, children select friends and ultimately someone's feelings get hurt.

Muscular Strength

Muscular strength is involved when a single muscle or group of muscles are used to apply force. According to Zaichkowsky, Zaichkowsky, and Martinek (1980, p.54) "Strength refers to the ability to exert force, such as lifting or pulling weight or lifting your own body." It is much easier and more common to develop strength in the lower body than in the upper body. Many everyday events such as walking and running and jumping on outdoor equipment are common activities that develop lower body strength. Unintentionally, there appears to be an abundance of activities that emphasize lower body strength with a tendency to neglect upper body development. Upper body development in modern society is usually weaker (Nichols, 1990). We appear to have developed children who have great fine motor control who exercise these parts of their bodies when they use the keyboard or the joysticks (Graham, Holt/Hale and Parker, 1993).

"Strength is not just how much muscle one has; it is an interaction of the number and size of muscle cells, the different ratio of fibre types in muscle, and the frequency with which muscle cells can be contracted." (Thomas and Thomas, 1988, p. 30) We suggest you encourage climbing on apparatus, ropes, trees, and monkey bars. To develop strength in younger children, you should provide push-pull toys and things to move and carry around. Older children should be encouraged to help move and set up equipment that will result in using the upper body. They should be encouraged to participate in a variety of manipulative sports and activities such as basketball, badminton, throwing and catching.

Play structures at the daycare or in the park around the corner can be used to increase children's level of physical fitness. If the structure has "monkey bars" encourage children to try and hold on for a few seconds without letting go, then as their upper bodies become stronger encourage them to try and move along the "monkey bars" swinging from rung to rung.

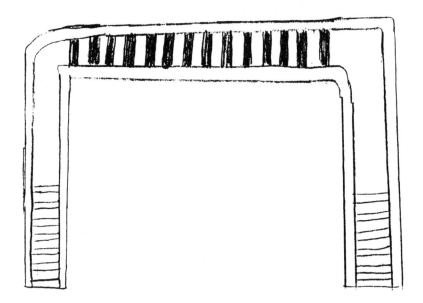

DRAWING 3.2. Upper body strength can be developed on the monkey bars. Perspective
by child age 10

Muscular Endurance

Muscular endurance is the ability of a muscle group to repeat an action over and
over for a sustained period of time.   "Muscular endurance is very important to motor
performance because most skills do not require a maximum effort; rather, they require
the movement to be executed repeatedly." (Thomas and Thomas, 1988, p. 30) High-level
training tends to rely on muscular endurance as a means of maximizing potential. The
repetitive arm action used in swimming the front crawl is an example of muscular
endurance. Lifting your legs over and over while hiking up a steep mountain is another
example.

Muscular endurance differs from muscular strength in that you can perform an
action once to demonstrate muscular strength, whereas muscular endurance requires
repeated actions. Follow any young child around as he learns to stand and walk. If you
were to stand and sit, sit and stand, as many times as he does, you would be exhausted.
He is demonstrating muscular endurance.

Studies indicate that there appear to be no gender differences in the level of
performance in this area until the age of eight(Gallahue, 1982). At around eight years
of age it seems that boys begin to fare better in this area relative to their female

counterparts. We believe that this to some extent is due to cultural bias and a tendency to focus on more active sports for elementary school age boys than for the same age girls.

Flexibility

This refers to the range of motion in the joints and varies with age and physical condition (Nichols, 1990). The degree of movement and range of motion that is possible in each joint is what influences flexibility. The joints are made up of connective tissue structures including cartilage and ligaments. As children grow and develop these connective tissues lose elasticity. It is the suppleness or elasticity of the joints that permits young children to be comfortable stretching into positions that adults are not comfortable with. For example, preschoolers appear comfortable sitting with their legs tucked behind them, whereas adults find this rather uncomfortable. Although children may feel comfortable in this position it is **contraindicated** as it puts tremendous pressure on the knee and hip joint.

According to Payne and Isaacs (1991), physical activity is necessary to maintain joint mobility. We can help children retain flexibility by having them stretch muscles at the end of movement sessions, while their muscles are still warm. Stretching muscles before warming up can lead to injury. Ideally it is important that children do some light movement to elevate the heart rate, sending oxygenated blood to the muscles, then do some light stretching before the activity and focus on flexibility only at the end. Warm-up exercises are very simple movements that involve the larger muscles of the body. They are mildly active, not strenuous in nature, and prepare the body for more energetic activity.

Fitness for Life

The only way to develop fitness for life is to make movement fun, exciting, and enjoyable. Physical fitness should be promoted both indoors and out. Planning a balance between the indoor and outdoor movement curriculum is often a challenge to the most experienced educator. North American climate is variable. Make the weather work to your advantage. Modify your activities so that they can be easily adapted to all that Mother Nature throws at us. For example, there is no reason not to bring out rubber balls in the snow or mats in the summer. Use rainy days for a good walk in the puddles.

Tedious repetition leads to boredom and lack of interest. Children are not interested in fitness goals, they want to have a good time. According to Cooper (1991) it is inappropriate to push young children into a fitness program that is developmentally beyond their capabilities. Develop activities that are at the right level for the children so that they do not become discouraged. Join in the fun and model appropriate behaviour. Let children know that you value fitness too. Make sure experiences are fun and keep the activity level high.

CHAPTER HIGHLIGHTS

Balance is an important factor in the child's ability to learn to move and to move to learn. The two types of balance are static and dynamic. Static balance is important when a person holds or amintains a position, while dynamic balance is called into play when a person is moving. The centre of gravity shifts as the body moves. The base of support includes those parts of the body that come in contact with a surface.

Physical fitness is important to everyone. It is an underlying principle of movement. It is crucial that all children develop a positive attitude toward physical fitness. Physical fitness includes cardiovascular endurance, muscular strength, muscular endurance, and flexibility. Cardiovascular endurance involves the heart and lungs, muscular strength is the power in a muscle, muscular endurance invovles muscle stamina, and flexibility is the range of motion.

LEARNING OPPORTUNITIES

1. ‖   <u>Chase</u>

    Age: three years and up

    Ratio: one to ten

    Procedure:

    A great outdoor game. A fun way to keep yourself and the children physically fit. Once you have the group together, or those children who would like to participate ready, tell them that you are going to start running and that they need to count to five or ten before they can start to chase you. It is also fun to have the children decide on a " base " where you can go when you need to have a break!! Remember the children will probably be able to run for a longer period of time then you will.

    Variation: Have one or two children be "it"

    focus: cardiovascular endurance

2. ‖   <u>Crazy Carpets</u>

    Age: three years and up

    Ratio: will vary depending on the age of the children

    Procedure:

    This is a wonderful outdoor winter activity. You need to wait for, or create, piles of snow. Take out your crazy carpets, climb up the hill, and slide down over and over again. It is climbing the pile or hill of snow that provides the children with a great opportunity to increase their cardiovascular endurance. (Crazy carpets are a rectangular shape of flexible plastic just large enough to sit on.**)**

    focus: cardiovascular endurance, muscular endurance

3. ‖ <u>Musical Balance</u>

Age: three years and up

Ratio: three to five years, one to eight
five to six years, one to ten

Procedure:

Children are encouraged to run around the room as they listen to fast-paced up-beat music. When the music stops they need to balance on one part of their body. For example, standing on one foot, balancing on one knee. Encourage the children to try and balance on different parts of their body each time.

focus: cardiovascular endurance, muscular strength, balance, auditory perception, directional awareness

4. ‖ <u>Freeze Tag</u>

Age: four years and up

Ratio: one to ten/twelve

Procedure:

One or two children are selected to be "it," depending on the size of the group. "It" is called the "wind." Another child is selected to be the "sun." The other children are referred to as the "water." When a child is touched by the wind, he must freeze on the spot. The child cannot move until touched by the sun. Give as many children as possible time to be the wind, the sun, and the water that freezes.

focus: static balance, cardiovascular endurance, directional awareness

5. ‖ <u>Action Ball</u>

    Age: six years

    Ratio: one to twelve

    Procedure:

    The children are initially divided into two groups with the playing area divided into two equal sections. There is a line down the middle. Put a large soft rubber or sponge ball into play. The members of one team direct the ball to gently hit the members of the other team. For safety reasons, hitting is below the knee only. If hit, the player changes teams and plays from the other side of the line. An individual must be hit before the ball bounces. If the ball is caught and not dropped, play continues.

    focus: dynamic balance, directional awareness,spatial awareness

REFERENCES

Adams, Williams C. (1991) *Foundations of Physical Education, Exercise and Sport Sciences.* Philadelphia: Lea Febiger.

Allsbrook, Lee (1992) "Fitness Should Fit Children," *The Journal of Physical Education, Recreation and Dance.* August 1992, pp. 47-49.

Cooper, Kenneth H., M.D., M.P.H. (1991) *Kid Fitness.* New York: Bantam Books.

Cratty, Bryant J. (1986) *Perceptual Motor Development in Infants and Children.* New Jersey: Prentice-Hall.

Gallahue, David L.[a] (1982) *Developmental Movement Experiences for Children.* New York: John Wiley and Sons.

Gallahue, David L.[b] (1989) *Understanding Motor Development, Infants, Children, and Adolescents.* New York: Benchmark Press Inc.

Gauthier, Pierre & Haman, Andrea (1992) " Physical Fitness," *Canadian Social Trends,* Summer, pp. 18-19.

Gerhardt, Lydia A. (1973) *Moving and Knowing.* Englewood Cliffs, N.J.: Prentice-Hall International.

Graham, George, Holt/Hale, Shirley and Parker, Melissa (1993) *Children Moving.* Third edition, Mountain View, California: Mayfield Publishing Company.

Kirchner, Glenn   (1992)   *Physical Education for Elementary School Children* (8th ed.) Dubuque, Iowa: Brown Publishers, 1992.

Lambert, Leslie T. and Grube, Paul E.   (1988)   "The Physical/Motor Fitness Learning Centre. Reston: Virginia. *Journal of Physical Education, Recreation and Dance,* March.

Nichols, Beverly (1990) *Moving and Learning.* St.Louis: Times Mirror.

Pangrazi, R.P. & Dauer, V. (1981) *Movement in Early Childhood And Primary Education.* Minneapolis: Burgess Publishing Company.

Payne, V. Gregory & Isaacs, Larry D. (1991) *Human Motor Development, A Lifespan Approach.* California: Mayfield Publishing.

Roberts, Scott C. & Staver, Pam (1992) " Fit Kids," *American Health,* September, pp.70 - 75.

Sanders, Stephen   (1992)   *Designing Preschool Movement Programs.* Champaign, Il.: Human Kinetics Books.

Segal,Julius, Ph.D. & Segal, Zelda (1992) " No More Couch Potatoes," *Parents Magazine* September, p.235.

Thelen, Ester (1983) "Learning to Walk is Still an *Old* Problem," *Journal of Motor Behaviour,* V. 15, No. 2, pp. 139-161.

Thomas, J.R., Lee, A.M. & Thomas K.T.   (1988)   *Physical Education For Children: Concepts Into Practice.* Champaign, Il.: Human Kinetics Books.

Williams, Harriet G. (1983) *Perceptual and Motor Development.* Englewood Cliffs, N.J.:Prentice-Hall.

Zaichkowsky, L.D., Zaichkowsky, L.B., & Martinek, T.J.   (1980)   *Growth and Development, The Child and Physical Activity,* St. Louis: C.V. Mosby Co.

PART II

DEVELOPMENTAL OVERVIEW

In this chapter you will learn about:

- Reflexes
  - immediate survival reflexes
  - other common reflexes
- Voluntary Movement
  - developmental direction
  - differentiation
- Infant and Toddler Opportunities
- Learning opportunities

FROM INFANT TO TODDLER

Infants participate actively in their world, both initiating engagement with others and responding to their invitations, both controlling others and being controlled by others.

LaVisa Cam Wilson

When children are born the majority of their motor actions are involuntary movements. As children grow and develop, there is a gradual shift from a predominance of involuntary movements to a predominance of voluntary movements.

It is not uncommon for children to begin their life at the daycare as young as six months of age. By that time, many reflexes will begin to fade, opening the door to more purposeful and controlled movements. However, many reflexes will still be present. We felt that a discussion on this early stage of development would not be complete without an explanation and description of some of the basic reflexes that all humans' experience. We have purposely used simple and concise language and although we discuss infant reflexes that are present at birth, learning opportunities offered begin at six months reflecting the earliest age that a child would be placed in a daycare environment.

As we discussed in Chapter 1, movement is both a learned and a maturational process. We will now elaborate on this maturational process as it evolves from infancy to toddlerhood. You can stimulate learning through movement during this early stage of development. A number of suggestions are provided in the learning opportunity section. Our discussion is limited to those reflexes that are seen in infancy and fade with time.

INFANT REFLEXES

The research into infant reflexes dates back to 1877 when Darwin first started to investigate this area of development. It was only in 1938 that researchers began to document and examine fetal movements in utero and include this period of development as part of the reflexive phase(Capute, Accardo, et al., 1978). The past twenty years has seen a surge in the interest and study of reflexes as a result of Piaget's findings based on studies of his own children. Studies have been carried out to determine if early fetal movements could be used as a predictor for later motor development. It is important to note that the research into reflexes has not been conclusive.

Some researchers feel that reflexes existed as part of our evolution as humans (Rosenbaum,1991), and at one time were necessary and that with changes in our society and environment, this is no longer the case. The grasp reflex described later in this chapter provides a good example of this. We believe that these involuntary movements are part of the child's development, provide evidence of patterning of later voluntary movements, and are therefore worthy of discussion. In fact, reflexes are inhibited prior to the appearance of their voluntary counterpart. Each reflex we discuss can be seen in some form of voluntary or *automated* movement after the reflex has disappeared. An automated movement is one that occurs voluntarily but without conscious thought. Walking is such a movement. We do not think about placing one foot in front of the other or adjusting our step to a change in surface. We simply perform the motor task at hand.

Reflexes and reflexive movements are studied for a variety of reasons. One reason, it is believed, is that infants store and internalize the information they receive from reflexes. This stored information is retrieved by them as they begin attempts at voluntary movement. Children begin to organize ideas about the world around by building on reflexes centred on *assimilation* (Livingston,1978). Assimilation is a perceptual process where information is taken in through sensory stimulation, filtered, and adjusted to fit with existing knowledge. Reflexes are not learned movements. They occur during the infant's first interactions with the environment as a primary means of information gathering. During the first months of life, infants can be observed making aimless movements with their arms and legs, spontaneously grasping an object, or for no apparent reason, grasping a finger that is put in the palm of their hand. Providing a stimulus such as stroking the side of the face will elicit a response whereby the infant will turn and search for the source of the stimulus. All these actions represent involuntary reactions in the presence of different stimuli.

This information processing stage parallels Piaget's first three stages of sensorimotor development. "Piaget think's the neonates reflexes are much like other schemas because they show assimilation and accommodation; profit from repetition and provide satisfaction. The only difference between reflexes and other schemas is that reflexes are innate".(Baldwin, 1980, p166) The reflexive phase of motor development should not be underestimated. It is during this sensorimotor period that the infant constructs cognitive understanding that will serve as a basis for later perceptual and intellectual development(Piaget & Inhelder, 1969). This level of cognitive understanding, which is constantly adjusting with new input, will be referred to as a base of knowledge or *knowledge base*.

Some initial reflexes, such as sucking, are essential in the first few months of life. Hence, the response to stroking the side of the face is seeking something to suck. Taking this one step further, an infant may start to associate sucking as pleasurable. As a result, she may at first accidentally find her thumb and find gratification sucking it. While thumb sucking is not a reflex, it was stimulated by the reflex and is known as a secondary circular response. This is followed by the tertiary circular response where the infant deliberately repeats a given behaviour, in this case, sucking. The infant begins to explore objects, such as a rattle or teething ring, by mouthing and sucking them. This deliberate sucking action evolved from a survival reflex. All reflexes provide some foundation for future knowledge. In some cases reflexes are needed for survival, in others they may be precursors to later voluntary movements. The presence or absence of a reflex at a given stage of development can serve as an indicator of normal healthy growth.

The unique characteristics of each individual will dictate variance in the rate of reflex inhibition and the development of controlled motor function. A vast majority of reflexes such as the tonic neck reflex, swimming reflex, and babinski reflex, to mention a few, fade out with time at different rates. Others, such as blinking, remain with us for life. Under normal circumstances, infant reflexes disappear, presumably as a result of neurological changes (Rosenbaum, 1991). Often when reflexes do not fad at the appropriate times they can signal neurological damage (Rosenbaum, 1991). If, for example, the moro reflex lasts too long, it will interfere with normal motor development. The presence of the babinski reflex in older children or in adults is an indication of neurological malfunction (Rosenbaum, 1991).

Reflexes are used as an indicator in the assessment of how well the central nervous system is functioning in the newborn. There are many tests in this area but they are beyond the scope of this book. We will provide the reader with a general overview of some of the basic and more common reflexes, identifying descriptors and why it is important to understand reflexes in general. We refer you to the reference section at the end of this chapter for further study in this area.

Immediate Survival Instincts

The reflexes described below represent the first way in which infants learn about their world. They include the survival and protection responses that are **subcortically controlled**. That is, they are controlled by the lower part of the brain. Life sustaining elements such as breathing are also subcortically controlled.

Rooting and Sucking

The rooting reflex is elicited by gently stroking the infant's cheek around the mouth. The infant will search for the source of stroking by moving her mouth and tongue in the direction of the stroking. If the infant finds the source of stroking she begins to suck. This reflex is essential for survival and contributes to a newborn's ability to take in food. The sucking reflex gradually develops into purposeful action.

It is difficult to determine if rooting and sucking actually disappear, are suppressed, or become incorporated into voluntary movement control(Keogh and Sugden, 1985). We know that this reflex is present at birth and becomes voluntary around four months of age (Allen and Marotz, 1989).

Other Common Reflexes

Where reflexes are concerned, there is a predictable sequence of infant development. At first there is an avoidance or withdrawal reaction to a stimulus. This may reflect an earlier evolutionary need for survival. With many reflexes, as with the babinski/plantar reflexes, this avoidance reaction evolves into a grasping one where the child moves towards the stimulus.

Most reflexes, including the sucking reflex described above, resemble or are considered as precursors to later voluntary movements. There generally seems to be a waiting period between the reflex, its disappearance, and the appearance of the voluntary action that resembles the earlier reflex. According to Field (1990, p. 46), "The normally dormant period between the early reflexes and the later voluntary behaviour may be necessary for other developments, such as motor control for better voluntary walking or eye-hand coordination for more finely tuned grasping."

Tonic Neck Reflex

The infant is placed in the **supine** position, that is lying on its back. The infant's head is turned to one side causing the arms on that side of the body to extend to the same side. The other arm will take on a flex position. This is often referred to as the *fencing position*. This reflex generally fades by about sixteen weeks (Allen and Marotz, 1989).

The tonic neck reflex can be used in the delivery of an infant. The arm reflexively extends on the same side that the head is turned. If need be, the physician or midwife can use the arm to guide the baby through the birthing canal. An interesting point to keep in mind is that this same reflex, so useful at birth, can inhibit normal rudimentary movements. If the hand and neck reflex stay too strongly linked, the infant will not be able to reach out independently.

There are voluntary movement patterns that resemble the tonic neck reflex position. The baseball catcher leaping in the air, reaching out to catch a fly ball (Rosenbaum, 1991) is one example. Another involves the tennis player as she reaches up to one side for an overhead smash. In both instances, the individual jumps up in the air and the head turns to the side of the approaching object. The arm and leg on the side opposite to the one reaching for the approaching object flexes upward and the body takes on a fencing position. This substantiates the claim that there is apparent pre-wiring of the nervous system.

Babinski and Plantar Grasp Reflex

These reflexes occur when the sole of the foot is stroked. In the babinski reflex this stroking results in the toes spreading open, moving away from the stimulus. The babinski reflex is present at birth, gradually fading away at around the fourth month of life. It is replaced by the plantar grasp reflex. The plantar grasp reflex is identified by providing the same stimulus but the toes flex or curl inward instead of outward.

Grasp Reflex (Palmar and Plantar)

Placing an object or finger in the palm of the infant's hand will cause her to close her fingers around the object presented. Once she has closed her hand around the object she is unable to " let go " or release the object voluntarily. This is one reflex where there does not seem to be a large time lag between the disappearance of the reflex and the voluntary movement of grasping.

If you subscribe to Darwin's theory of evolution, the plantar grasp reflex, previously referred to along with the babinski reflex, may be regarded as a remnant from a time when our ancestors lived in trees (Rosenbaum, 1991).

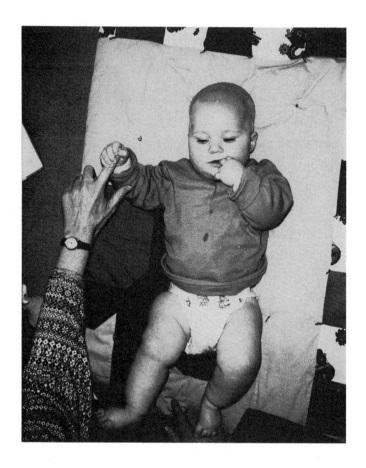

Photo 4.1. Grasp Reflex

Moro Reflex

This reflex can be activated by the same stimulus as the startle reflex described below. Firstly, if the infant is held in the air in a prone position, then suddenly lowered, the moro reflex will occur. As a part of the infant's protective mechanism she will respond by raising her arms and flinging the legs out in an avoidance reaction. She then pulls back towards her body. The second way to trigger this reflex is through the presence of sudden noise(Rosenbaum, 1991).

Startle Reflex

The startle reflex occurs months after the moro reflex has disappeared. The child quickly flexes her arms and legs bringing them in towards her, in response to the same stimuli described above. In either case, touching or holding the infant is an effective way to calm her.

Walking or Stepping Reflex

This reflex is stimulated by holding the infant upright, feet touching the ground or a flat surface such as a table. The infant responds to the pressure by engaging in stepping actions. The stepping action, is present at birth, seems to disappear at four weeks of age and reappear at eight months. There are two strong and opposing explanations of this. Zelazo (1983) in his research hypothesized that the reappearance of the stepping reflex is due to simultaneous development of cognitive sequencing abilities. The control of this stepping action leads to walking, which requires this cognitive sequencing.

We concur with Thelen (1983) who on the other hand suggests a very different view. She says that cognitive sequencing does not bear relevance since mentally handicapped people can walk. Further, she states that in fact there is no disappearance of the reflex. Her research findings indicate that when three-or four- month-old babies were submerged in the water, in an upright position from the waist down, the stepping begins. This suggests that babies' legs between two and eight months are not strong enough to support their heavier bodies and that in a more buoyant state the reflex is present.

Interestingly, this stepping action resembles a pushing away of the surface, which is in effect an avoidance reaction. We do not suggest exercising the child as a means of getting her to walk more quickly. On the contrary, we advocate that educators follow the natural developmental rhythm of each child.

Their "mere presence is an indicator of how deeply locomotor activities are rooted within the nervous system" (Gallahue, 1982, p.138). All reflexes appear to pre-wire some form of voluntary human movement.

Crawling and Swimming Reflex

These two reflexes resemble each other. One takes place on land while the other occurs in the water. The crawling reflex happens before the infant can walk. Placed in the *prone* position (lying on the stomach), the arms and legs extend alternatingly as if crawling.

This swimming reflex appears when the infant is placed in the prone position on or in water. The infant responds by carrying out rhythmic swimming motions. It must be noted that the infants placed in water cannot yet keep their heads up. This must be done for them. This reflex usually disappears by the fifth month.

Labyrinthine Righting Reflex

This interesting reflex is not present at birth. It appears at around two months of age and becomes stronger by about six months. It is therefore one that you will probably see in a daycare environment. It is important with respect to the contribution it makes towards an upright head and body position (Cratty, 1986). What happens is that if you tilt the infant to the side or tilt her back, she will try to keep her head up and centred. Placing the infant in a prone position on a large ball and rolling the ball gently from side to side will provide the infant with opportunity to experience this reflex in a positive environment. This reflex is an important one in the mastery of gravity and is needed in the first months and year of life (Cratty, 1986).

In general, it is important for educators to have a good knowledge of reflexes in order to identify their absence or presence at a given stage of development. According to Fogel(1992), reflex stimulation provides social interaction, guided use of language, and opens the door to infant play. He further implies that repeated opportunity for the infant to experience reflex stimulation may influence the timing of emergence of neural pathways needed for voluntary movement. Experience may affect the facility with which those pathways are motivated.

Figure 4.1. offers a guide of approximate ages at which most reflexes are present and at what age they generally fade. The information presented is meant as a quick visual reference and is based on an amalgamation of information from Fogel(1992), Cratty(1986), Allen and Marotz(1989), and Rosenbaum(1991).

REFLEX	STIMULUS	APPROXIMATE AGE REFLEX APPEARS	APPROXIMATE AGE REFLEX FADES
sucking and rooting	stroke side of face gently	birth	3 - 4 months
tonic neck	infant's head is turned to side	birth	4 - 5 months
babinski	upward stroke to the ball of the foot	birth	4 months
palmar grasp	place object in palm of hand	birth	6 months
plantar grasp	stroke the sole of the foot	birth	6 months, usually disappears by first year
moro	infant held prone in air and suddenly lowered	birth	9 months
startle	same as above or at presence of sudden noise	birth	8 months
swimming	place infant on top of water, hold head up for air	birth	6 months
stepping or walking	hold infant upright with feet touching ground	birth to 4 weeks	8 months to 1 year
labyrinthine righting	tilting body to side as on body ball	2 months	1 year(partially fades) some aspect of righting reflex remains throughout life

Figure 4.1. Timing of reflex appearance and disappearance

VOLUNTARY MOVEMENT

Developmental Direction And Differentiation

In Chapter 1 we defined the law of developmental direction, differentiation, and motor refinement. In this section we look at how the theory translates into specific movements you will see. Towards the end of the first month of life infants begin to respond to their environment with controlled movements. The first signs of voluntary movement are slight, including only movements of the head, neck, and eyes (Payne & Isaacs, 1991). During this period of infancy there appears to be significant overlap in both involuntary and voluntary movements. The timing and the emergence of motor reflexes and controlled movements varies from child to child but the sequence of development is predictable and predetermined. Timing can be affected by genetic make-up as well as cultural influences. Each infant's development is dependent on her unique rate of growth, experience, and readiness for learning.

One of the most complicated tasks infants need to accomplish after birth is that of gaining and maintaining a sense of balance or equilibrium and of acquiring control of their own movements. These two tasks, identified in Chapter 3, proceed according to developmental direction and differentiation. Cephalocaudal development is evidenced in the labyrinthine righting reflex which provides initial response of balancing the head. This later translates into purposeful head control that most humans are capable of.

Gaining control of the head and neck muscles encourages the infant to lift her head and visually explore the world around. The human body is fascinating in its efficiency of skills for at about the same time as infants gain postural control over their head position (around two months) they also experience marked improvement of visual perception and cognitive organization (Fogel, 1992). In essence, physical strength and visual ability improve simultaneously.

Each time the head is lifted, the muscles around the neck and spine area are exercised, which in turn assists in developing the back muscles. The back muscles strengthen contributing to the child's ability to sit up. The arms are used and strengthened as infants lift their upper body to explore the world around.

Differentiation is witnessed when we look at an infant who swipes at objects before being able to voluntarily and accurately grasp them. These examples of motor achievements represent the rudiments of voluntary movement. Simple observation will show each of us that "the ability to sit comes before the ability to crawl, and the ability to crawl comes before standing and walking"(Johnson and Johnson, 1984, p.138). Some infants completely bypass the crawling stage. They do not get up on their hands and knees that follows the Law of Developmental Direction and cephalocaudal development. They rock back and forth as if ready to take off, however the rocking does not translate into crawling.

An infant's motor growth is nothing short of incredible during the first year of life. She goes from interacting with her world first from a horizontal position, to rolling over from front to back and back to front, to a sitting position, and finally to a standing or vertical position.

There are times when it appears that the infant accomplishes many motor tasks. At other times there may appear to be lags in these milestone achievements. These lags may be completely normal and are not cause for alarm. These can occur as a result of a change in sleeping or eating habits, or simply as a result of concentrating on a newly acquired skill to the exclusion of an already accomplished skill.

Your most important function is to provide the infant with an environment that enhances and encourages development. The infant's environment should allow for freedom of movement, but be safe and unrestricted. There should be room for the infant to move around and explore with her body. An infant will eagerly grasp, mouth, look at, and explore what is provided.

Infants are attracted to moving objects. Mobiles are appealing to the infant who is stationary or just beginning to move. As the infant sits up and is more mobile, rolling a ball may be an effective motivator. A developmentally appropriate environment will allow the infant to develop and practise her movement skills and learn about the world around. Educators should remember that as infants and toddlers develop and acquire new movement skills, they need to be provided with ongoing opportunities to continue practising previously acquired ones.

For example, when the toddler has just learned to walk, we often expect her to stop crawling. This can be frustrating and upsetting for the child. First steps take a lot of concentration and effort. Crawling may still provide an easier and faster way to get around. The toddler's new skills should be recognized but she should be made to feel secure in the knowledge that old skills are still valid. We all know how to run, but practicality dictates that we spend more time walking.

CHAPTER HIGHLIGHTS

Our discussion on infancy through toddlerhood has shown that in the course of normal development many, if not most, reflexes disappear before the infant reaches the toddler stage. We have discussed thirteen reflexes in this chapter. They are the sucking, rooting, tonic neck, babinski, moro, startle, palmer and plantar grasp, walking, stepping, swimming, crawling and the labyrinthine righting reflex. They all represent involuntary movements. The nervous system assimilates involuntary movements as it matures. This enables the child to control movements in a voluntary manner (Beaty, 1990).

The first voluntary movements of infancy are commonly called rudimentary movements. These rudimentary movements are the foundation on which all fundamental movements are based. They are in fact the beginning of purposeful motor actions and are the topic of discussion for the next chapter.

CHECK	**CHILD'S AGE IN MONTHS**	**OBSERVATION**
_____	_____	*lifts head when placed in prone position*
_____	_____	*rolls onto back when placed on stomach*
_____	_____	*rolls on stomach when placed on back*
_____	_____	*when placed in supine position, will raise legs off ground*
_____	_____	*sits unassisted*
_____	_____	*gets up on hands and knees*
_____	_____	*rocks back and forth on hands and knees*
_____	_____	*pulls self to standing*
_____	_____	*follows moving object (ocular control)*

FIGURE 4.2. Body control (designed based on personal observations and references at the back of this chapter)

	CHILD'S AGE	
CHECK	**IN MONTHS**	**OBSERVATION**

CHECK	IN MONTHS	OBSERVATION
_____	_____	*reflexively grasps objects that are placed in the hand*
_____	_____	*swats objects that are suspended*
_____	_____	*plays with hands and feet*
_____	_____	*purposefully grasps objects*
_____	_____	*clumsily reaches for objects*
_____	_____	*transfers objects from one hand to the other*
_____	_____	*releases objects held in hand voluntarily*
_____	_____	*reaches for objects with relative accuracy*
_____	_____	*holds objects using a palmer grasp*
_____	_____	*holds objects using a pincer grasp*
_____	_____	*can pick up an object using a pincer grasp*
_____	_____	*carries objects while crawling, cruising, or walking*

FIGURE 4.3. Hand Control (This checklist was designed using reference texts listed at the end of this chapter)

INFANT AND TODDLER OPPORTUNITIES

Planning gross motor and fine motor opportunities for the infant and toddler needs to include a variety of elements. You should provide the child with a safe environment that gives her the opportunity to explore and manipulate the treasures that surround her. Children need to be dressed in the least restrictive type of clothing, thus allowing them the greatest freedom to move. Curriculum planning for the infant and toddler will also vary depending on the child's degree of mobility. Depending on whether the child is sitting, creeping, or standing the focus on the type of opportunities and material may vary. As well there are certain pieces of equipment that are functional with all levels of development, such as balls. Some all time favourite activities include "Ring Around the Rosie" and "Head and Shoulders." These songs can be played together with the children before they can stand to carry out actions.

Equipment such as mats to roll around on, balls of various sizes, trikes and tractors to ride, toys that can be pulled or pushed, a small object or set of stairs to climb, and a tunnel to crawl through, are all valuable pieces of equipment to have for children of this age range. These do not require any special gymnasium setup and will provide meaningful opportunities for exploration, simply because they are available. Nonbreakable mirrors are another valuable piece of equipment. As children come down a slide or climb over a mat they enjoy watching themselves in the mirror. They can feel the movements that their body is accomplishing and see how their body is moving.

It is important to observe the developing infant/toddler and recognize motor achievements resulting from motor differentiation. The ages given are meant as approximate guidelines only. By about the fourth month, the infant can usually hold its head quite steadily. Anytime between the fifth and twelfth months one should start to observe the infant begin the process of sitting. The first attempts at sitting usually have the child sitting on the floor bent over at the waist with her two hands out in front for support. As the child starts to maintain her balance in this position, they will gradually take one hand away. This is a great accomplishment as it allows the child to use her free hand to explore the things around her. With time you will notice that the child no longer needs her hands for support and that when she sits up she appears to be stable and well balanced with a straight back. Anywhere from the fifth month on the developing child will use objects such as furniture or push-pull toys to aid in standing. (The fifth month is early for this skill.) You should not insist or expect these milestones as achievements, rather provide opportunities for practise through your classroom design.

LEARNING OPPORTUNITIES

1. ‖ <u>Wrap Around</u>

> **Age**:   six months
>
> **Ratio:**   one to one
>
> **Procedure:**

> Place a small rattle in the palm of the infant's hand. Her fingers will wrap around the rattle. Learning through movement occurs resulting from her sense of touch as her fingers are clenched on the rattle. The action of closing her hand around the object will also serve to strengthen her hand muscles as she reflexively maintains a grip on the object. When the infant spontaneously moves her hand the rattle will shake and produce a sound, introducing an auditory stimulus. Through this one, although seemingly simple activity, the infant is provided with a variety of stimulus sources and opportunities to learn through movement.

> focus: grasp reflex, tactile perception

2. ‖   <u>Little Tommy Tittle Mouse</u>

    Age: six months to twelve months

    Ratio: one to one

    Procedure:

Sit on the floor with your knees bent toward your chest (feet are flat on the floor). Place the child on top of your knees holding her around the waist or under the arms. Sing the following song:

> Little Tommy tittle mouse sat upon a pole
> Wiggle waggle, wiggle waggle   *sway the child from side to side*
> Fell into a hole   *separate your knees and while holding onto her let her drop gently down between your legs.*

focus: auditory perception, balance

3. ‖   <u>The Grand Old Duke of York</u>

    Age: six months to twelve months

    Ratio: one to one

    Procedure:

Sit in the same position as in the above activity and begin to sing the following song with accompanying actions.

> The Grand Old Duke of York
> He had ten thousand men
> He marched them to the top of the hill
>   *move feet in a marching motion*
> And he marched them down again
>   *move legs down till they are flat on the floor*
> When they were up they were up
>   *move feet & knees up to gain to original position*
> And when they were down they were down
>   *move legs down*
> And when they were only half way up
>   *move legs halfway*
> They were neither up nor down
>   *slide legs up and down*

focus: directional awareness, auditory perception, balance

4. ‖ <u>Row, Row, Row Your Boat</u>

    Age: ten months and up

    Ratio: partner activity

    Procedure:

Sit on the floor facing the child. As the two of you hold hands, make sure your feet are touching. Sing "row, row, row your boat." while moving backwards and forwards as if rowing a boat. Once the child has the idea, she can easily play this with a friend.

focus: auditory perception, balance, flexibility

5. ‖ <u>Jump Jump Look Who's in the Box</u>

    Age: twelve months to twenty-four months

    Ratio: one to six

    Procedure:

You and the children crouch down as if inside a jack-in-the- box. Begin to sing "Look, look, look who is in the box. It's Elana." When Elana hears her name she jumps up as if jumping out of the box and continues to jump three or four times. In a large group, call out more than one name at a time and have a few children jump together.

focus: auditory perception, balance, cardiovascular fitness

6. ‖   <u>A Climbing We Will Go</u>

Age: twelve months and up

Ratio: adult is present for supervision

Procedure:

Infants and toddlers love to climb. The most readily available piece of equipment in your environment for climbing is stairs. Far too often we close off our stairs as we see them as being dangerous. Why not leave the first few stairs available for climbing and just block off the remainder of the stairs. You can also provide a variety of apparatus for the child to conquer. For example, a rocking boat turned over is great for mastering wide graduated stairs. Another option is a small slide that gives the child the opportunity to climb up and slide down, only to begin again.

focus: cardiovascular fitness, balance, muscular strength

REFERENCES

Allen, Eileen K. and Marotz, Lynn (1989) *Developmental Profiles, Birth to Six.* Albany, New York: Delmar Publishers Inc.

Anselmo, Sandra (1987) *Early Childhood Development, Prenatal Development Through Age Eight.* Columbus, Ohio: Merrill Publishing Company.

Baldwin, A.L. (1980) *Theories of Child Development*, 2nd edition. New York: John Wiley.

Beaty, Janice (1994) *Observing Development of the Young Child* third edition. Don Mills Ontario: MacMillan Publishing Company.

Capute, Arnold J., Accardo, Pasquale J., Vining, Eileen P.G.; Rubenstein, James E. and Harryman, Susan (1978) *Primitive Reflex Profile.* University Park Press.

Cratty, Bryant J. (1986) *Perceptual and Motor Development in Infants and Children.* New Jersey: Prentice Hall.

Cowan, Phillip A. (1978) *Piaget With Feeling.* New York: Holt Rinehart and Winston.

Charlesworth, R. *Understanding Child Development*, 2nd edition.   Lousiana: Delmar Publishing, Louisiana State University.

Curtis, Sandra (1982) *The Joy of Movement in Early Childhood.* New York: Teachers College Press.

Field, Tiffany (1990) *Infancy.* Cambridge: Harvard University Press.

Fogel, Alan (1992) Movement and Communication in Human Infancy: The Social Dynamics of Development. *Human Movement Science* (11)387-423.

Gallahue, David L. (1982) *Understanding Motor Development in Children.*, New York: John Wiley and Sons.

Johnson & Johnson (1984) *Your Baby, The First Wondrous Year.* edited by: Chase, Richard A., Fisher, John J. III, Rubin, Richard. New York: Collier MacMillan.

Keogh, Jack and Sugden, David (1985) *Movement Skill Development.* New York: MacMillan Publishing Company.

Livingston, Robert B. (1978) *Sensory Processing, Perception, and Behaviour.* New York: Raven Press.

Maxim, George W. (1989) *The Very Young* 3rd edition. Columbus: Merrill Publishing Company, Westchester University.

Mena-Gonsalves, Janet & Windmeyer, Diane (1989) *Infants, Toddlers, and Caregivers.* Mountain View, California: Mayfield Publishing Co.

Owens, Karen (1987) *The World of The Child.* Holt Rinehart and Winston, CBS College Publishing.

Payne, V. Gregory & Isaacs, Larry D. (1991) *Human Motor Development, A Lifespan Approach.* California: Mayfield Publishing.

Piaget, Jean & Inhelder, Barbel (1969) *The Psychology of the Child.* New York: Basic Books Inc.

Rosenbaum, David A. (1991) *Human Motor Control.* San Diego, California: Academic Press Inc.

Smolak, Linda (1986) *Infancy.* Englewood Cliffs, New Jersey: Prentice-Hall.

Thelen, E. (1983) Learning to walk is still an "old" problem: A reply to Zelazo. *Journal of Motor Behaviour,* 15 (2) 139-161.

Weiser, Margaret (1991) *Infant Toddler Care and Education,* 2nd edition. New York: MacMillan Publishing Company.

In this chapter you will learn about:

- Fundamental movements
- Nonlocomotor skills
  - axial movements
  - stretching
- Locomotor skills
  - creeping, crawling and climbing, cruising
  - walking and running
  - leaping, hopping, and jumping
- Combination skills
  - galloping, skipping, and chasing
- Learning opportunities

FUNDAMENTAL MOVEMENTS:
NONLOCOMOTOR AND LOCOMOTOR SKILLS

Preschool and primary grade children are involved in the process of developing and refining fundamental movement abilities in a wide variety of stability, locomotor, and manipulative movements.

David Gallahue

FUNDAMENTAL MOVEMENTS

Conscious efforts by children to move their bodies in the way that they want to marks the beginning of fundamental movement skills. The basic fundamental movement skills include nonlocomotor, locomotor, and manipulative skills. These form movement building blocks that are required for sports performance, specialized motor tasks, and increased efficiency towards activities of daily living. In essence, fundamental movement skills are component parts that combined and refined, are required for sport, dance performance, and everyday movements.

The fundamental skills of nonlocomotion, locomotion, and manipulation are executed with the use of either the larger muscles or smaller muscles of the body. When the larger muscles are called into play we say that these skills are carried out using **gross motor abilities**. When smaller muscles are used, we say that **fine motor abilities** are at work. Gross motor and fine motor abilities represent broad labels of physical abilities.

Most locomotor and nonlocomotor skills fall into the category of gross motor abilities. Many manipulative skills fall into the category of fine motor abilities, with obvious exceptions such as throwing, catching, kicking, trapping, and trapping large objects. The topic of manipulation is explored further in the next chapter. In Figure 5.1. we provide a diagrammatic breakdown of the fundamental movement skills and some of the movement components of each category.

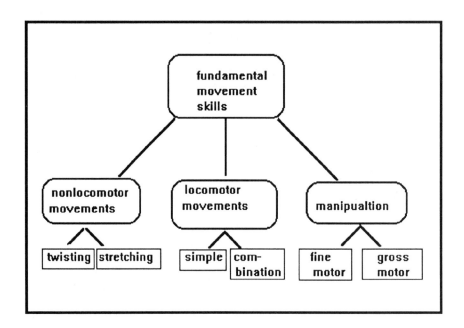

FIGURE 5.1. Fundamental movement skills and their components

The more children move "the more coordinated and complex their movement becomes"(Waite-Stupiansky, 1992, p.32). That is to say, in any given skill area, repetition expands a child's base of knowledge. The more often a skill is practised, the more automatic a response becomes. For example, when we learn to walk, steps are shaky and tentative. New terrain or an incline to walk over presents a challenge to the child who must carefully think each step. Adults, proficient at walking, can move forward without prethinking each step. They can also adjust to an icy patch on the sidewalk or climb up a small hill without much thought about foot placement. The skill of walking has become very automatic. Through experience, a motor pattern is learned and both physical and cognitive knowledge have been expanded.

The following anecdote provides an example of how motor play helps children test their own physical limits and improve fundamental motor skills. In this example, the child engages in **repetitive play** and she challenges and improves her ability to jump. Repetitive play involves testing a motor action by trying it over and over again as a means of learning about one's own physical limits and abilities.

♦♦♦

> *We were in the park today. Most of the children were running around the large equipment. Joelle noticed the climbing structure. It had three broad steps leading to a flat, long platform. Joelle climbed up the three steps and came down again. Each time she got to the top she would look down as if to jump, but would return down the steps the way she had come. On the third try she looked down, and then jumped. Pleased with her success, she continued to climb and jump, becoming more motorically confident and assured with each attempt.*

♦♦

It is only through appropriate and sufficient planning of motor activities that you can help children expand their knowledge base and subsequently reach their potential physical development. It is important that you provide a balance of open-ended play opportunities and games that do not eliminate the players. Open ended play refers to situations where equipment is either made available or set up and children are given the freedom to move about and use the equipment independently. Typically, the children who are eliminated first are the ones who could benefit the most from practice and experience. This is discussed in greater detail in Chapter 9. Children moving together interact with each other. This necessitates communication, sometimes pair work and sometimes group work. All this fosters a climate of positive growth in the psycho-social domain.

It is physical success that will encourage a child to achieve culturally normative skills. Wall (1982) defines culturally normative skills as those that are used by the majority of the people in a certain culture at a certain age. For example, North Americans seem quite obsessed with ball sports such as baseball, football, hockey, or soccer. Far Eastern culture has a greater affiliation to body control sports such as Tai Chi and the martial arts. These **phylogenetic** behaviours represent an important part of motor learning for physical success in any given culture. Basic fundamental skills discussed throughout this chapter are learned by all of us, regardless of culture. Developmental skills common to all, regardless of cultural and environmental influences, are referred to as **ontogenetic behaviours** and develop through a natural growth process. You should strive to present both developmentally appropriate and culturally relevant opportunities.

Figure 5.2. presents a visual representation of ontogenetic and phylogenetic behaviour and the implication for movement.

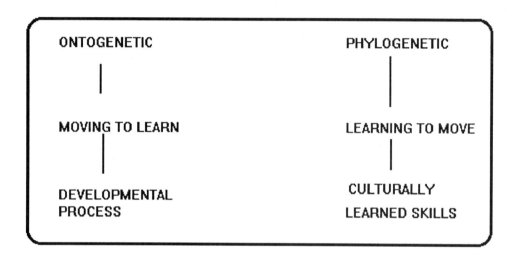

FIGURE 5.2. The ontogeny and phylogeny of movement

Equipment at the early stages of fundamental movement skills should be set up so that there is easy access to free exploration and a minimum of educator intervention during these exploratory periods. A detailed discussion on planning and equipment set-up can be found in Chapter 8. As mentioned earlier, trial and error experiences provide optimal learning. Through movement experiences children expand their knowledge base both physically and intellectually. Giving them time to solve their own problems and determine their best way to perhaps climb over an apparatus or under it provides invaluable opportunity for growth, learning, and creativity. "One of the methods by which all of us solve problems is to stumble on a solution without deciding ahead of time that it was a solution....Hence, we try something and see if it works."(Baldwin, 1980, p.176) Solutions to motor problems lead to motor success. Good motor performance in turn leads to good self-esteem. This in turn leads to a positive attitude towards physical activity and acceptance by peers, creating a positive learning cycle.

NONLOCOMOTOR SKILLS

In **nonlocomotor** skills all or part of the body may move but the individual does not actually travel from one place to another. Nonlocomotor skills include axial movements of bending and twisting, actions such as swinging, stretching, and reaching. Axial movements involve actions that change the body's position at the waist. Many ideas for developing nonlocomotor skills are explored in the chapter on creative movement.

As the body shifts positions, the centre of gravity must be adjusted, showing evidence of the importance of the underlying principles of balance. Many movement activities use a combination of static and dynamic balance as discussed in Chapter 3. Static balance is evidenced in a game of hot potato where each person turns from the waist in one direction to retrieve the object from the person beside them. In order to pass the object to the person on the other side, the body must change position but at no time actually changes location.

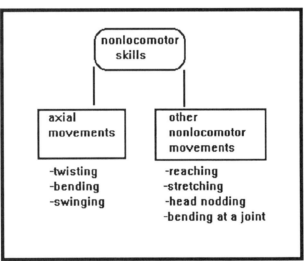

FIGURE 5.3. Some nonlocomotor movements

All nonlocomotor tasks involve dynamic balance while the body is shifting position. Although you may physically stay in one spot in nonlocomotor tasks, your body is moving, perhaps up and down, or twisting and bending. Each of these actions dictates that the body's centre of gravity will shift.

There are some simple materials you can set out during free play in order to effectively develop nonlocomotor skills. You might arrange large foam blocks in the preschool environment to promote bending and lifting, carrying and arranging. Older children can be given opportunity to prepare the outdoor environment in the spring. Give them wheel barrels and earth to prepare the ground for planting. Not only are they bending, twisting and lifting, but they are also taking pride in their environment.

You can also encourage nonlocomotor skills by providing guided activities. These permit creativity and variance as far as the child's motor output is concerned, but are generally led by the educator. Learning Opportunities such as Statue Game, Human Machine, or Sculptures in My Garden, are but a few examples.

LOCOMOTOR SKILLS

Locomotor skills involve physically travelling from one point in space to another. This includes moving horizontally as well as vertically. Locomotor skills, like non-locomotor ones, bring into action static and dynamic balance. Again, static balance is relied on as the body stops between different movements. A good example of how static and dynamic balance work together in locomotor skills is seen in the game of basketball or tennis where a player must stop before changing direction.

Becoming mobile marks a major achievement in life. This mobility brings a whole new world within reach. Children can see, explore, and experience new things that were before out of their grasp. They have learned to move and this will help them move to learn. Children first propel themselves by moving across the ground while flat on the floor. They will flip over from back to front and front to back, first by accident and then with purposeful intention. This gives them a view of the world from two perspectives, lying on their stomach in the prone position and lying on their back in the supine position. As children gain control of their bodies and can sit up, they will be able to move about in an upright position. Some children will scoot about on their bums as a means of getting around.

Before standing, comes a range of movements known as creeping and crawling. Although these two major motor achievements occur during the infant and toddler years, we felt they are better discussed here as part of the sequential acquisition of locomotor skills.

Creeping

This movement can be described as the action of pulling oneself along the floor while flat on the stomach. The arms reach forward and pull the body, the legs push off with the knees and toes. The torso does not lift off the floor. This progression respects cephalocaudal development and is usually visible by about seven months of age (Keogh and Sugden, 1985).

This is a cumbersome way of moving about but a very important stage in purposeful locomotor movement. Children feel the floor with every part of their body. Through tactile perception children take in the texture of the surface. If the room is warm enough, take off as much of their clothing as possible so that they can use their sense of touch to heighten exploration and learning. We especially suggest letting them move around with bare feet so that their toes can assist in their movement.

Crawling

Crawling is described as moving about in the environment while on hands and knees. Often it is preceded by rocking. Children get up on their hands and knees and rock many times before figuring out that moving forward will not cause a loss of balance. There are some children who miss this stage of development. Controversy surrounds this area and whether or not it is important for neurological organization to pass through this skill. Some believe it is necessary for hemisphere dominance (Delacato, 1966, Meiste Vitale, 1985), while others believe there is a lack of evidence to draw any conclusions(Gallahue, 1982). Crawling involves much the same arm and leg patterns as creeping. The essential difference is that the torso is lifted off the ground.

There are ways to encourage crawling in the young child.

♦ ♦ ♦

> *Doug, aged 10 months, would not crawl. Very efficient at pulling himself about on his stomach and scooting on his bottom, he felt no need to crawl. Jason, the educator, decided to move the gate away from the entrance to the stairs and place it three stairs up. This created a safe space to crawl up,with the body torso supported on the stair below. As Doug reached the top stair and slid down, Jason would raise the gate to the fourth stair. Soon, the skill of crawling was mastered on the stairs and was transferred to the floor.*
>
> ♦ ♦ ♦

Climbing

This skill involves exactly the same movements as crawling. For this reason we have decided to discuss this movement outside of its developmental order. The only difference is that we crawl on the horizontal plane and we climb on a vertical plane. Climbing requires considerably more upper body and general strength than does crawling. When climbing we are always climbing on something, such as stairs, a ladder, or even a mountain. When climbing we are always pulling our weight against the force of gravity. Children love to climb up trees and, if you watch carefully, you will notice how they pull themselves up with their arms, then push off with their feet.

Homolateral and Contralateral Actions

In creeping, crawling, and climbing, there can be **homolateral** or **contralateral** actions. Homolateral actions involve an arm and foot moving in synchrony on the same side of the body. The right arm and right leg both move forward before the left leg and left arm do. In contralateral action, the right arm will move forward, then the opposite leg, then the left arm, and finally the right leg. In other words, the limbs move in opposition to each other.

There is some interesting documentation on the importance of going through this stage of contralateral movement and the effect on development of the left brain and right brain. We refer you to Meiste Vitale's (1985) book listed at the end of the chapter for reference in this area.

As children move onwards and upwards, new and exciting ways of moving about or locomoting occur. The child may **cruise**, by holding on to a wall or a piece of furniture while shuffling their feet in an effort to move along sideways. This extends the horizon of the child's world. When in an upright position the child's eye level is in a different place.

Walking

The first walking steps are very shaky. The torso almost seems to move ahead of the legs and children will commonly take a few steps, then lose balance. Another interesting point to note in the child's development of walking is the way in which the hands are used. Initially you can observe the hands and arms above the child's head to help maintain balance. As balance improves, the arms start to lower until they are beside the body with normal arm swing in opposition to the legs.

Children begin to walk using an immature, wide stance. Steps are very short and there is a flatfooted contact with the surface (Gallahue, 1982. b, Rosenbaum, 1991). The knees are slightly bent and the toes may point outwards. As they become more proficient at walking, the legs come closer together. Table 5.1. provides a general checklist to assist in observing the skill of walking in young children.

CHECK	CHILD'S AGE IN MONTHS	OBSERVATION
_____	_____	*walks using wide base of support*
_____	_____	*uses flatfooted action*
_____	_____	*uses heel-toe action*
_____	_____	*arms are held up high for balance*
_____	_____	*arms swing with alternating action to leg*
_____	_____	*walks up incline*
_____	_____	*walks down incline*
_____	_____	*walks upstairs with assistance*
_____	_____	*uses same lead leg to go upstairs*
_____	_____	*uses alternate lead leg to go upstairs*
_____	_____	*walks downstairs assisted*
_____	_____	*walks downstairs unassisted*
_____	_____	*uses same lead leg to go downstairs*
_____	_____	*uses alternate lead leg to go downstairs*

TABLE 5.1. Checklist of walking progression. [Information extrapolated from Keogh and Sugden(1985), Pangrazi and Dauer (1981), Allen and Marotz (1989), and Rosenbaum (1991)].

Walking represents the first fundamental locomotor skill that does not require the assistance of one or both hands in travelling from one place to another. Although it is true that a toddler can carry an object while crawling, walking represents the first time the hands are truly free for other tasks. What a marvellous achievement!

Walking is generally used to propel the body in a forward direction. However, we can walk backward or sideways, or even on our tiptoes. You can use long steps or short tiny ones. In stair climbing, children adjust their step pattern to environmental demands (Keogh and Sugden, 1985). Terrain can also influence the type of step or gait used in walking (Rosenbaum, 1991). We can see how perceptual feedback cues play an important role (Powers, 1989) in the adjustment of step pattern.

Opportunity to practise the skills of cruising and walking will help refine them. There are many wonderful push pull-toys on the market that can and should be provided. There are also some readily available materials and homemade toys that can be extremely effective at this time. For example, children delight in pushing around a lightweight chair or pulling a large, grocery bag. To ensure safety, use only paper bags.

Running

Running at times resembles fast walking. It appears to have many of the same characteristics. Running, like walking, involves a heel-toe action. The heel makes contact with the ground first, then the centre and finally the front of the foot. The heel lifts off the ground first with a push off from the ball of the foot and the toes. A common problem observed in young children involves a tendency to run on their toes only, never putting the heel of their foot down. This action should be corrected by providing opportunities for the children to get their whole foot down. Walking in the sand is helpful as it forces the whole foot down.

Photo 5.1. Two year old child running.

There is always a flight phase between steps. This becomes possible with increased strength and balance. In this flight phase, there is an instant when both legs are off the ground between steps. In the early stage of running the feet are rather flat-footed and there is a limited flight phase. This means that the whole foot lands more or less at the same time when making contact with the surface below. Gradually the flat-footed run develops into the mature running pattern with a heel-toe action. As in the early stages of walking, the child's upper body seems to want to go ahead of the legs. Often this can result in a loss of balance. The mature run is accompanied by a slight forward lean of the torso (Graham et al., 1992).

Arms swing back and forth in opposition to the leg movements. In the initial stages of running the arm movements are stiff and have a short swing (Gallahue, 1982(a)). The length and fluidity of the arm swing gradually increases. A mature running pattern has elbows bent almost at a 90 degree angle. "Running is an important fundamental motor skill, for without a good fundamental running pattern, the capacity of and/or opportunity for the child to successfully participate in many physical activities is limited. Running and variations of running are essential components of most games and sports"(Williams, p. 213).

Jumping

Jumping is a two-foot takeoff and two-foot landing. Children should be given opportunities to jump up and down, up to a low object, down from an object, as well as over objects. Poor coordination of the arms and legs is a common developmental problem. For example, in the early stages of jumping, the arms do not seem to assist the takeoff. They stay beside the body rather than thrusting upwards. At about five or six years of age you will notice that the arms swing upwards first, initiating the actual jump.

A common difficulty children seem to have is in forgetting to bend their knees on the landing. They often lock their knees. The educator might suggest a game where the children could touch their toes as soon as they land. This will help them focus on the task that will ultimately encourage the knee bend. Jumping skills can be practised in many ways. Some simple games include Five Little Monkeys and Water Jumps.

Leaping

Leaping can be described as a one foot takeoff and opposite foot landing. Both legs are off the ground at the same time. The arm opposition is the same as in a run but a leap requires much more force than a run (Graham, Holt/Hale, Parker, 1992). With school age children you can give verbal cues and use imagery to help them leap high or far. If you want to encourage height, suggest that children try to touch the sky when they takeoff. If you want to focus on distance, suggest that the children try to leap over an imaginary river or towards the wall at the other end of the room.

Hopping

This is a one foot takeoff with a landing on the same foot as the takeoff. Hopping involves an upward projection of the body, but you can hop forward, sideways, or backward. It is easier for a child to take off from one foot successfully than it is to land on the same foot. Initially the free leg comes down for balance and support. This is a normal developmental progression.

At about three or four, children have difficulty carrying out many hops in sequence. By about five or six they are generally capable of consecutive hops.

COMBINATION SKILLS

These involve the combination of two or more simple fundamental skills. Children need to first master simple fundamental skills before they can be expected to combine movements.

Galloping

This step is a combination of a step and a hop with the same foot leading all the way through. Initial weight of the body is taken by the lead foot as it comes in contact with the landing surface. The back foot closes in quickly to meet up with the lead leg (Graham et al., 1992). In a gallop, the body is propelled in a forward direction employing a syncopated rhythm.

Skipping

Skipping is also a combination of a step and a hop but the lead foot alternates. This should not be taught per se as children will do it in their own good time. Teaching or directly telling a child how to skip will only frustrate him. There are numerous approaches that will encourage skipping. Provide music or a drumbeat that has the syncopated rhythm of a skip pattern, have one child skip next to another who has already mastered the skill, or have a child who can skip hold hands and skip with the child who has not developed the rhythmic motor pattern. Partner work can be carried out in the form of a game, whereby every time the music stops, children all must take a new partner. Focusing on the step or directly teaching it will not be as effective as modelling.

Chase

A chase is a side step with a hop added, or a gallop to the side. This is a tricky move to learn but children enjoy games and dances that include this funny way of moving sideways. A simple game to play with six - and seven - year old children is to tell them to pretend they are like a pirate with one wooden leg. That leg cannot bend while sliding to the side.

CHAPTER HIGHLIGHTS

To summarize, nonlocomotor skills are performed in one place, always involve moving the body, and require dynamic balance. Nonlocomotor skills can occur in many positions, standing, sitting, or lying down to (mention a few). Think about how you can move some of your body parts while remaining in one place.

Locomotor actions involve gross motor movements and require the body to move in space. Many open-ended materials can be provided for independent exploration. These will be discussed in the chapter on planning. Hoops can be placed on the floor to jump in and out of. Blocks of different heights can be used to jump from. These are all safe materials that require relatively little supervision, making great opportunities for free play set up both indoors and outdoors. Younger children sometimes need less intense supervision because they do not have mastery of the skills and take less risks. Older children, more secure in their fundamental skills, tend to be more adventurous, taking greater risks.

A general locomotor checklist is provided on the following page. It can be used separately or in conjunction with other checklists throughout the chapter.

	CHILD'S AGE	
CHECK	**IN MONTHS**	**OBSERVATION**

CHECK	AGE	OBSERVATION
_____	_____	*creeps: pulls self along floor while flat on stomach*
_____	_____	*scoots: in sitting position, uses arms to push self along floor*
_____	_____	*crawls: on hands and feet*
_____	_____	*crawls: on hands and knees*
_____	_____	*cruises: moves laterally while holding on to an object such as a table*
_____	_____	*creeps up or downstairs*
_____	_____	*walks two or three steps without support*
_____	_____	*walks without holding on to anything*
_____	_____	*walks upstairs*
_____	_____	*runs*
_____	_____	*jumps on the floor*
_____	_____	*jumps from an object*
_____	_____	*hops but nonlanding leg touches the ground upon landing*
_____	_____	*hops and keeps nonlanding leg in the air*
_____	_____	*hops two or three times consecutively*
_____	_____	*gallops*
_____	_____	*skips*

* NOTE: This checklist is based on personal observations and readings from the list of books provided in the reference section.

TABLE 5.2. General locomotor checklist.

LEARNING OPPORTUNITIES

1. ‖ Statue Game

   Age: three years and up

   Ratio: one to eight

   Procedure:

   Select music of your choice. Sharon, Lois, and Brams's, "The Statue Game" or Sandy Offenheim's album "If Snowflakes Fell in Flowers" are possibilities. Play the music and randomly stop it. When the music stops the children must all freeze and strike a pose, pretending to be a statue. When the music resumes, they are once again free to move. Ask children to freeze in a very stretched out position, in a very curled up position, to freeze while bending at the waist, and so on. Make up your own directions, encouraging axial movements.

   focus: nonlocomotor and locomotor movements, dynamic and static balance

2. ‖ Five Little Monkeys

   Age: three years and up

   Ratio: one to five

   Procedure:

   Set out thick mats on the floor --- a wedge mat is fun if you wish to add a different dimension to the jumping. Standing on the mat with a group of children chant the following:

   Chant
   Five little monkeys jumping on the bed,
   One fell off and bumped his head,
   Mamma called the doctor and the doctor said
   No more monkeys jumping on the bed.

   Actions
   Jump up and down on the mat for verses 1 and 2. On verse 3, stop making sure your knees are bent, pretend to phone. On verse 4 point to the group as you repeat what the doctor said.

   Repeat the chant and the actions as long as there is interest.

   focus: locomotor movement of jumping, dynamic balance

3. ‖   Sculptures In My Garden

> **Age:**   six years and up
>
> **Ratio:**   one to ten
>
> **Procedure:**
>
> Group the children in pairs. One child is designated as the sculpture and the other the artist. The sculpture is instructed to either stand in one spot or to lie down on the floor. The artist moves the limbs and torso of the sculpture to create a statue. Soft music is used to set the tone. New age music is particularly suited for this type of exercise.
>
> focus: bending, twisting, stretching, balance

4. ‖   Water Jumping

> **Age:**   seven years and up
>
> **Ratio:**   one to eight
>
> **Procedure:**
>
> This exercise is carried out in a swimming pool. Hollow hoops are set to float in the deep end. Children are asked to jump into the hole of the hoop. Note: children should be able to swim or have appropriate floatation devices on.
>
> focus: jumping, cardiovascular endurance

5. ‖   Snake

> **Age:**   four years and up, variation # 1
>   eight years and up, variation # 2
>
> **Ratio:**   variable
>
> **Procedure:**
>
> Variation # 1: Have the children form one long line, holding onto the waist of the child in front of them. Instruct the children to remain attached throughout. The front of the line is the head while the back of the line is the tail of the snake. The tail is given a scarf that is loosely attached to someone's back. On the signal, the front of the line has to run to catch the tail at the back of the line ensuring that the snake never breaks loose.

Variation # 2: (Kirshner, 1992) This is a more competitive version of the game. The rules are the same except there are two teams. The tail of each team has a scarf. The head of one team tries to grab the tail of the other team.

tail X X X X X X   heads O O O O O O   tail

focus: running, cardiovascular endurance, bending

REFERENCES

Allen, Eileen K. and Marotz, Lynn (1989) *Developmental Profiles, From Birth to Six.* Albany, New York: Delmar Publishers.

Baldwin, A.L. (1980) *Theories of Child Development*, 2nd edition. New York: John Wiley and Sons Inc.

Delacato, C. (1966) *Neurological Organization and Reading.* Springfield, Illinois: Charles C. Thomas.

Gallahue, David L.(a) (1982) *Developmental Movement Experiences for Children.* New York: John Wiley and Sons.

Gallahue, David L.(b) (1982) *Understanding Motor Development in Children.* New York: John Wiley and Sons.

Gallahue, David L.(c) (1989) *Understanding Motor Development, Infants, Children, Adolescents.* Benchmark Press Inc.

Graham, Holt/Hale, Parker (1992) *Children Moving: A Reflective Approach to Teaching Physical Education.* Mountain View, California: Mayfield Publishing.

Keogh, Jack and Sugden, David (1985) *Movement Skill Development.* New York: MacMillan.

Kirschner, Glenn (1992) 8th edition. *Physical Education for Elementary School Children.* Dubuque, Iowa: Wm. C. Brown Publishers.

Lay-Dopyera, Margaret & Dopyera, John (1991) 4th edition. *Becoming a Teacher of Young Children*, New York: McGraw Hill.

Malina, Robert & Bouchard, Claude (1991) *Growth, Maturation, and Physical Activity.* Windsor, Ontario: Human Kinetics Publishers Inc.

Meister Vitale, Barbara (1985) *Unicorns Are Real, A Right Brained Approach To Learning.* Rolling Hills Estates, California: Jalmar Press.

Pangrazi, Robert P. & Dauer, Victor P. (1981) *Movement in Early Childhood Education.* Minnesota: Burgess Publishing Company.

Payne, V. Gregory & Isaacs, Larry D. (1991) *Human Motor Development, A Lifespan Approach.* California: Mayfield Publishing.

Powers, William T. (1989) *Living Control Systems.* Gravel Switch: Kentucky. The Control Systems Group, Inc.

Rosenbaum, David A. (1991) *Human Motor Control.* San Diego, California: Academic Press Inc.

Waite-Stupiansky, Sandra (1992) "Let's Go Outside," *Scholastic Pre-K Today.* May/June, pp. 31-34.

Wall, A.E. (1982) Physically Awkward Children: A Motor Development Perspective. In J.P. Das, R.F. Mulcahy, and A.E. Wall(Eds.) *Theory and Research in Learning Disabilities*, pp.253-268, New York: Plenum Press.

Williams, Harriet (1983) *Perceptual and Motor Development.* Englewood Cliffs, New Jersey: Prentice-Hall.

▬▬

In this chapter you will learn about:

- Gross motor manipulation
  - throwing, catching, ballbouncing
  - trapping, kicking, striking
- Fine motor manipulation
  - corralling, swatting,
- Eye-hand and eye-foot coordination
- Learning opportunities

MANIPULATIVE SKILLS

From this rudimentary beginning his perception of time space relationships improves, and he becomes capable of attempting more challenging tasks.

Ralph Wickstrom

Learning to control and manipulate objects is a complex skill. It involves the self and the manoeuvring of an object. It is this control of objects that distinguishes manipulation activities from nonlocomotor and locomotor ones. Successful manipulation of objects is very dependent on an individual's eye- hand and eye-foot coordination, as well as on manual and tactual experiences related to the object that is being manipulated.

Eye-hand and eye-foot coordination refers to the coordination between the hands or the feet and visual cues. There is an interaction between sensory and motor processes (Winstein and Schmidt, 1989). The physical element of sight and the perceptual element of interpretation of the environment are involved in eye coordination (Gibson, 1966). It is both the interpretation of what children see and how their body reacts based on the visual cues that helps them to succeed at a manipulative task (Williams, 1983).

Eye-motor coordination is important to the success of an abundance of skills, yet for some reason we often neglect to plan specifically for its development. Planning can be as simple as setting out opportunities such as stringing beads, puzzles, or organizing a game of soccer or tennis.

In general, ball games develop eye-motor coordination quite effectively. If someone throws a ball to you, you need to first judge the distance between you and the ball and adjust the position of your body to accommodate the direction and speed at which the ball is coming. Your movement response is based on visual interpretation of the moving object. Your reaction to the moving object involves a keen sense of timing (temporal awareness). Another factor influencing the way in which you react to a moving object relates to the weight, size, and texture of the object. You first must see the ball coming toward you and perceive its size, weight, and speed of travel in order to adjust yourself to the task of catching.

Tactual experiences help children acquire the knowledge of size, shape, texture, and weight of an object. This knowledge then becomes a source of stored information. For example, manual exploration of a toy provides input through the hands while tactual experiences help the child develop the sense of an object by how it feels.

As with all fundamental skills, manipulation can use fine and/or gross motor abilities. Fine and gross motor manipulative skills like other motor learning follows a predetermined developmental sequence. These skills are also dependent on developmental direction and differentiation. As differentiation of motor skills occurs children become more capable of using the small muscles of their hands in a more refined way. They will use a palmar grasp to pick up a large object, such as a block, before successfully picking up the smaller item, such as a pencil, which requires the use of a pincer grasp. It also means that children are able to catch a large ball using a bear hug with their whole arm before being capable of writing their name with a refined pincer grasp.

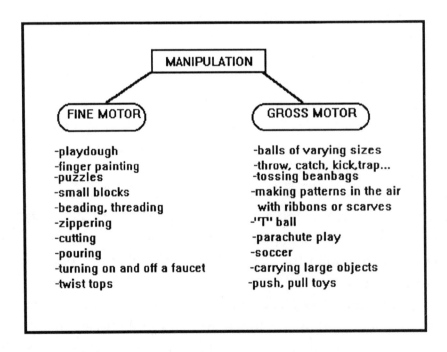

FIGURE 6.1. Fine and gross motor manipulative activities.

Development of motor skills between the ages of three and five is rapid (Gallahue, 1982).   Between five and seven there are still rapid improvements in eye-motor coordination, but the rate of growth is slower than it was in the years from three to five. It is important to offer tasks that will develop eye-motor coordination through both fine and gross motor skills as there is a transference in this visual coordination ability.   See Figure 6.1. for a few ideas in planning manipulative activities.

GROSS MOTOR MANIPULATION

Gross motor manipulation involves the use of just about any body part, but is most often thought of in terms of the hands and the feet. In throwing and catching the hands come in direct contact with the object being manipulated. Kicking involves direct contact of an object with the feet, while in trapping and striking just about any body part comes in direct contact with the object. At the mature stage of gross motor manipulative skills, the whole body is usually used in the production of force and in assistance with balance and stability.

Trapping

Trapping is a skill often associated with soccer. In recent years in western culture this sport has become very popular with children as young as four years old. Trapping can be done with any body part that can stop the momentum of an object. The key to this skill is the ability to stop the force of a rolling or tossed object. This of course can be done while sitting, standing, staying still, or moving. Challenge the children you are working with to find fun ways to trap a rolling ball.

One way to stop the force of a rolling ball is by using the feet while in a standing position. Children can use one or both feet to stop the momentum of a ball that is coming in their direction. When children are first learning how to trap a ball they place their foot out to stop the ball but often their foot goes past the ball and misses. This is because their eye-foot coordination is not yet refined. Children can also trap the ball with two feet. Here neither foot leaves the ground. The feet form a "V" with heels touching and the ball is trapped in this position.

Hands can also be used to trap a ball that is being rolled. This we will see is a pre-requisite skill to catching. In this situation trapping occurs when an individual receives the force of a rolled ball and stops its momentum by placing the arms or hands on top of the ball. This first attempt at trapping may resemble a bear hug around the ball. Toddlers and young children should be encouraged to practise trapping a ball as someone rolls it to them. You can do this with younger children in a sitting position, while older children may have more fun running after a rolling ball and stopping it with their hands.

A tossed ball can be trapped as well. Think of the game of soccer where the goalie uses any and all body parts to trap the ball. This ability requires advanced eye-hand and body coordination.

Throwing

Throwing was probably first developed during a primitive time in our history when we had to hunt for food for survival. This skill is used today in many professional sports. It is interesting to observe the difference in a child's first attempts to throw versus the pattern used by a professional athlete. The initial throwing motion uses the whole arm and appears somewhat clumsy when stepping into the throw, whereas athletes use their whole body to assist in putting momentum and accuracy into a throw.

"Although a child might demonstrate sudden accuracy in throwing, for example, acquisition of this skill likely took place in small steps beginning with primitive swiping and grasping in infancy" (Trawick-Smith, 1994, p 243). The first attempts at throwing are really more of a flinging type motion with no goal or direction in mind. Although there is some connection between releasing and throwing, releasing is seen as a fine motor task while throwing is seen as a gross motor task. Picture releasing by thinking of the toddler standing in the crib with a look of delight on her face as she drops every toy out. As the child continues to practise this action, movements become more refined and resemble the skill of throwing. In releasing, the object is dropped and in the early stages of throwing, the object is sent downwards instead of forward.

There are many variations to throwing, such as overhand, underhand, and sideways. Children have the capacity to throw with one hand or two and should be given a chance to experience both. As they are developing the skill of throwing, they usually begin by throwing overhand with two hands and underhand with one. A common problem in throwing is a loss of balance in the forward action as the ball is released. Most of us will all be able to throw relatively well as a result of the maturational process. However, the refined skill of throwing requires a lot of repetition. By the middle of the preschool years, some instruction should be provided in the form of guidance as to correct procedures in executing a particular skill. These should be given in the form of positive suggestions such as, *"Why not try it this way...?"* or *"What would happen if...?"*.

In working on developing the skill of throwing, children will find it easier to throw small items such as beanbags rather than larger ones such as a large ball. Holding onto a beanbag is simpler because it is lightweight and does not put the child off balance. It fits nicely into the palm of the hand.

DRAWING 6.1. A schoolage child's rendition of throwing and catching.

Catching

Catching is a skill that is often associated with throwing. They seem to go hand in hand. Catching is however a more complex skill than throwing. It requires greater emphasis on eye-hand coordination and relies on visual tracking. Eye-hand coordination is an important component in developing the skill of catching and will improve through experiential opportunities. Tracking or following a moving object and pinpointing where it will stop is a complex task. A moving "object is no longer a static picture of a moment in time; it is constantly changing and thus requires continuous perceptual reorganization" (Keogh and Sugden, 1985, p.289).

There are several prerequisite skills that children need to practise in order to help them reach the mature level of catching. These include such skills as **fetching** and trapping. As with catching the skills of fetching and trapping both stop the momentum of a moving object. Fetching is something toddlers especially have a lot of fun with. It is quite simply running after a ball and stopping its momentum before picking it up. This ability to fetch a ball and grasp it works to develop and prepare the finger and hand muscles for catching. As young children's visual tracking skills are not yet fully developed, it is difficult for them to pinpoint exactly where a rolling ball will stop. Simply permitting children to run after a rolling ball helps develop the co-requisite skill of visual tracking. Catching differs from trapping in that the momentum of the object is stopped by the hands only and is held onto for a brief moment of time.

As is the case in the learning of most new skills, experience with prerequisite skills can be helpful and less intimidating. When children are ready to explore catching they will have an easier time catching larger rather than smaller balls. You may recall that this is the reverse to the sequence of throwing that was discussed earlier. The early stages of catching will resemble a scooping motion. It is also important to remember that children often need verbal reminders in the beginning stages of catching. For example it's a good idea to say to them: "watch," "keep your eye on the ball," " here it comes." These verbal cues are effective ways for you to help the children focus on the ball. Very often in the initial attempts at catching children will turn the head away from the object as if they are afraid of being hit. We can only assume that with experience they learn and develop a sense of trust towards the person who is throwing the object and as their ability to judge the timing and distance of the ball develops they will become less fearful. For this reason, we suggest that the speed with which the ball is thrown be adjusted to correspond to the individual level or stage that each child is at. This will help maximize the young child's visual tracking.

When the child is first introduced to catching it is important to work with her on an individual basis. Provide challenges that the child will be able to manage so that she will be encouraged to extend learning.

Ball Bouncing

We have all played games involving ball bouncing. Often, a more sophisticated version of ball bouncing is referred to as dribbling. It is common in such sports as basketball.

Ball bouncing begins very simply when the ball is released by the child and it rebounds off the floor. This does not represent purposeful bouncing. The purposeful action of bouncing requires that the hand make contact with the ball after it rebounds off the ground and propels the ball back down. The hand pushes the ball down into the ground. Children have great fun just bouncing and chasing a ball for the sake of it.

Some balls have a harder bounce and move with greater velocity, while others rebound more slowly. You might want to experiment with the balls that you have access to in order to determine which ones to use on any given occasion.

Kicking

Children are natural kickers, they kick for pure pleasure. Anyone who has been pregnant has experienced the reflexive kick of a budding athlete. Think too of the child walking along a path that has twigs and pebbles and rocks lying along the way. What does the child do? She kicks the objects as she walks along.

DRAWING 6.2. Preparation, kick, and follow through.

Kicking involves imparting force to an object to propel it forward. The beginning stages of kicking can be described as a pushing or nudging motion. Toddlers can often be seen pushing a ball along the floor. Gradually they start to swing at the ball. They can often be observed swinging their foot back in anticipation of kicking the ball. Sometimes, their foot goes right by the target, or they kick the ball and then lose their balance and fall down. They understand the concept of kicking; however, their eye-foot coordination doesn't allow them to hit their target, and they are still developing their sense of balance. Kicking requires the ability to maintain balance on one leg while the other leg is lifted off the ground to impart force to an object. According to Wickstrom (1977), kicking represents the "only form of striking in which the arms do not play a direct role." This may be an oversimplification as the arms are very important to balance and, in the mature pattern, there seems to be an automatic extension of the arm forward as the leg is pulled to the back. Perhaps we could say the arms are used primarily for balance and do not come in direct contact with the object.

As is the case with catching, children will have an easier time kicking a larger ball than a smaller one. The first activities involving kicking skills should be ones where the children are kicking a stationary ball. Gradually as this skill and visual tracking skills improve, children can be introduced to kicking a moving ball. Ultimately, distance is achieved by kicking through the ball.

Striking

Striking is a skill that is found in many different sports. It involves applying force to an object to send it away from the body. This can be performed with or without an implement as an extension of the body.

DRAWING 6.3. Striking, by a five year old child.

The first sports that probably come to mind are tennis and baseball. However the skill of striking is not only involved in all racket sports, such as badminton and squash, and other sports, such as golf and hockey, but it includes using parts of the body to strike objects. Each of the sports mentioned uses an object as an extension of the arm to add a sports challenge to the fundamental skill of striking. You will notice that young children will naturally begin to swat or bat objects such as mobiles placed over the crib. These are the rudimentary movements of striking.

Before the concept of striking is introduced you should provide opportunities to encourage the children to use their arms and hands in order to improve timing and visual accuracy. For example, it is important that children have the opportunity to swat such objects as balloons or beach balls. We suggest balloons as they are lightweight and slow moving thus giving the child the opportunity to track them and be successful at striking. A tether ball, or a homemade version of one is an excellent object to have hanging, not only in the classroom but outside as well.

The next step in the developmental progression is to introduce a piece of equipment as an extension device. Children should first be introduced to short handled pieces of equipment and then progress to larger pieces. They should first learn to strike a stationary object before being expected to strike a moving object. For example, you could have balloons hanging down at their eye level so that they will be able to reach and strike them.

Next, you might consider a progression with which to introduce the skills used in baseball. Start off with " T" ball, where the ball is placed on a pole. The child stands beside the ball on its "T," and swings the bat in order to hit the ball as far into the playing field as possible. Once this skill of striking stationary objects becomes sufficiently refined, the child can move on to striking moving objects, as in the game of baseball.

FINE MOTOR MANIPULATION

During the early years there is an overlap in fine and gross motor development. The process of proximodistal development dictates that a certain amount of gross motor development is needed before children can begin to develop fine motor manipulative skills. Some experiential knowledge early in the child's development is useful in the control and movement of the total body as a foundation for the development of refined hand and limb control used in fine manipulative tasks (Williams, 1983).

Integration of visual cues plays an important role in the development of hand coordination and accuracy of achievement towards successful execution of a manipulative task. For example, a child must successfully integrate visual skills with hand coordination in order to reach for an object. In closing the hand around an object there is an interrelationship between spatial cues, visual information, and fine motor skills (Laszlo and Bairstow, 1985). In studies with children from five to ten years of age, Laszlo and Bairstow (1985) found that children under six lack the spatial programming necessary to trace objects or colour within the lines accurately. This skill generally appears in children over six. For this reason, it is not wise to present tracing activities and colouring within the lines to children in the preschool years. This would only lead to frustration and serve to limit creativity.

The fine motor abilities are involved in the development of the pincer or palmar grasps. They include such refined tasks as beading, threading, buttoning, painting, or writing (to mention a few). Fine motor manipulation and the use of the hand muscles begins with the very young infant. Within the first four months of life, infants are demonstrating a crude grasp of objects (Allen and Marotz, 1989). The first manipulative skills that can be observed include reaching, grasping, and releasing. An infant's first attempts at reaching and grasping are usually unsuccessful. If you are sitting with an infant on your lap and there are objects within the line of vision, you may notice the infant begin to reach for these objects. At first the infant will miss, coming within a few centimetres of the target. This is usually due to a lack of eyehand coordination and perceptual development. This lack of success at reaching and grasping a target in infancy is so normal that it even has a special name. It is referred to as **corralling.**

The first grasping behaviours that we observe infants engaging in are reflexive movements. Gradually, as the infant develops, these reflexes fade, leaving room for voluntary grasping. As long as the involuntary reflex is present the development of voluntary action is inhibited (Lefrancois, 1973).

In the early months of life you can observe infants trying to grasp those objects that are within their line of vision. Once successful, the infant will hold onto the object very tightly. Although she can grasp the object, she has not yet developed the control necessary to release it. She does not have within her control the skill to relax her muscles. This skill will develop as the muscles in her hands mature.

The first type of grasp that the infant can be seen using is the palmar grasp. To recap our discussion from Chapter 4, this grasp can be described as holding an object with the whole hand. It is a rather crude and unrefined grasp. You should provide the child with objects to hold of varying sizes and textures. Children should also be encouraged to hold objects in both hands, together and/or separately. When passing an object to a child, alternate between the two sides of the body. Successful experiences with fine motor tasks help the toddler increase the level of independence. For example, while holding objects, the child will move them, turn them, twist them, look at them, and put them in the mouth. These actions assist the development of the muscles in the fingers and wrists. Once again, the child learns through movements of the self and objects. Many examples that are part of the daily routine come to mind. The toddler self-feeding or playing with finger foods are some examples during the early years. This usually starts out as quite a mess! Be patient, support her, and assist her towards independence and the development of fine motor skills. Older children enhance fine motor tasks through everyday life experiences such as tying shoes or brushing teeth.

Fine motor development does not just occur during planned fine motor activities. Routine tasks of dressing, eating, and clean up all provide the opportunity to practise. Children should also be able to explore and be exposed to opportunities that will allow them to refine fine motor skills in order to become competent to meet the increasing challenges presented in our environment.

Fine motor control is both sequential and predictable in its developmental patterns, yet we often do not see each step in the developmental progression of fine motor skills. The child seems to wake up one morning, magically capable of zippering a jacket or buttoning a shirt. "Actually, motor development is characterized by a gradual refinement in abilities; steps towards mastery of a particular skill are many although each step is often imperceptible" (Trawick-Smith p. 243). You can help by providing something new to strengthen and develop the muscles of the hands for the next challenge.

There is quite a diversity in the types of fine motor tasks that children attempt and these require them to use their hands in a variety of ways. For example, children hold brushes while painting at the easel. In this situation the hand is actually held up in the air against the easel. In piling up large blocks the hands work very differently. They wrap around the object in a looser more open grip, grabbing and releasing the object. In writing, the hand rests on a table or support.

Some fine motor activities require the use of only one hand. This is referred to as **unilateral** movement. This use of one hand or another contributes to the development of preferred hand (Williams, 1983). Unilateral tasks include primitive reaching and grasping actions as well as more refined tasks, such as holding a glass and lifting it up to drink. Most fine motor activities require the use of two hands performing the same task, such as in turning a jump rope, or performing different tasks with one hand complementing the other. In stringing beads for example, the two hands work to complement each other by performing slightly different fine motor functions. There is also twisting a cap off a jar, one hand turns the top and the other stabilizes the jar. The use of two hands simultaneously to perform different or same tasks is referred to as **bilateral** coordination (Williams,1983).

In most bilateral tasks we can see a tendency for one hand to dominate the task while the other acts to assist towards task completion. As certain fine motor tasks are accomplished, others are refined and developed resulting in isolation of specific movements. For example, in some fine motor tasks, such as typing or writing, there is greater use of the hand and wrist muscles and less dependence on whole arm movements.

Your role is very significant towards the development of fine motor skills. You need to develop a sense of when it is appropriate to introduce new fine motor challenges and provide a variety of materials and opportunities. By understanding and respecting the sequence of any particular task and providing opportunities that respect a progression from simple to complex, you play a valuable role in assisting children towards becoming proficient with fine motor tasks.

Use checklist 6.1. to record a fine motor profile of the development of the children in your group. In table 6.1., we provide a sequential progression to facilitate the development of cutting skills. Tearing is a simple way to divide paper into pieces. It can be introduced to children in the toddler years. Cutting play dough is fun for toddlers and younger pre school age children. Snipping paper with scissors is something generally introduced by age two to two and a half, but we suggest you use your observations as a guide for readiness. Once you have tried the cutting sequence, we invite you to design your own progression for other skill areas.

CUTTING SEQUENCE

1.	*Tearing paper. Provide children with paper to tear using both hands.*
2.	*Easy to cut materials. Provide children with materials that cut more easily than paper. These include playdough and plasticine. Cutting these types of materials gives children greater opportunity to practise the skill of opening and closing the scissors.*
3.	*Snipping paper with scissors. At first the educator or a child can hold the paper still for the other child who is cutting. Another option is to tape long strips of paper to a table. This enables the child to concentrate only on the cutting hand.*
4.	*Give the children many opportunities to cut paper. Magazine pages are easier to cut than conventional paper. (It is a good idea to tear the pages out of the magazine so that the children can rotate the paper as they cut, thereby simplifying their task.)*

TABLE 6.1. Sequential activities to enhance the fine motor skill of cutting.

The hands are also used as a means to take in information from the outside world. Above, in Step 1 of the cutting sequence, the fingers pinch the paper. It is the sense of touch that delivers the message to the brain as to whether the paper is rigid or soft and whether the tearing requires a strong forceful action or shorter smaller movements, using the whole arm.

It is true that the hands do not represent the only means to take in information through the sense of touch, but they do play an important role. Touch represents the *active perception* of the environment (Gibson, J.J., 1966). The hands can curl around an object and identify it at times without assistance of visual cues. The hands and fingers can determine the size, shape, texture, or weight of an object.

It can be noted that drawing generally precedes writing (Rosenbaum, 1991). By looking at children's drawings over the course of their development, you will notice a dramatic improvement in fine motor output. This is a result of increased fine motor control, improved spatial awareness, and perceptual and cognitive ability. Following is a checklist of a more or less sequential nature of the acquisition of fine motor skills. Writing implements can be thick crayons, more suitable for younger children, to thin pencils, more suited for the older children. Use Checklist 6.1. to record a fine motor profile of the development of the children in your group. Generally, you will notice many different ways that children hold their writing implements. This varies with age and stage of development.

GENERAL CHECKLIST

CHECK	CHILD'S AGE IN MONTHS	OBSERVATION

_____	_____	uses palmar grasp when holding objects such as blocks, crayons, duplo
_____	_____	uses pincer grasp when picking up objects
_____	_____	uses whole hand to wrap around writing implement
_____	_____	uses pincer grasp to hold writing implement
_____	_____	inserts objects using thumb and finger, e.g., peg into pegboard, puzzle pieces
_____	_____	uses both hands to connect building toys or pull them apart
_____	_____	strings objects together
_____	_____	can turn or twist lids off jars
_____	_____	pours from one container to another
_____	_____	can string medium size beads
_____	_____	can string small beads
_____	_____	cuts, holding scissors with two hands
_____	_____	cuts, holding scissors in one hand
_____	_____	in cutting, wrist position is turned in towards body
_____	_____	in cutting, wrist and hand point forward
_____	_____	can cut curved and/or rounded lines
_____	_____	dominant hand _____left _____right

* NOTE: We suggest using this checklist for children age two and up. For younger children refer to the checklist on hand control provided in Chapter 2.

CHECKLIST 6.1. Fine motor manipulation

CHAPTER HIGHLIGHTS

All manipulative skills can best be developed and reinforced through a variety of exploratory (open-ended) activities, guided opportunities, and games. In the earlier years we feel that it is extremely important to provide an abundance of exploratory activities, giving young children a maximum of time to learn at their own pace and in their own way. Guided opportunities permit the educator to interact in a positive and nonthreatening environment and to offer suggestions for improved performance, while focusing on the process and not the outcome. Once children develop their manipulative skills and master a basic level of personal success they can transfer skills to a game situation. Games should be played and introduced for the purpose of positive social interaction, and to practise and refine skills.

It can be very frustrating to the child if you introduce games that require catching and throwing before the child is developmentally ready. Providing children with a good selection of equipment and time to explore will benefit the child to the greatest extent. We sometimes forget simple ideas, like giving each child in the group a ball and letting her run off into open space to see what she can do with it. The children will toss it, bounce it, roll it, kick it, and create games with friends playing nearby.

The schoolaged child will also be interested in exploring objects but will spend less time exploring and more time developing or working towards a goal. Children enjoy shooting "baskets" on an individual basis but they also enjoy the challenge that a scrimmage will provide.

LEARNING OPPORTUNITIES

1. ‖ Roll the Ball

>   **Age:**   two and a half
>
>   **Ratio:**   one to eight
>
>   **Procedure:**
>
>   The children are sitting in a circle with their legs
>   in a "V" shape. You start to roll the ball and sing the following song:
>
>   Roll, roll, roll the ball
>   Roll it to a friend
>   Roll it back, roll it forth
>   Let's try this again.
>
>   (sung to the tune of Row Row Row Your Boat)
>   You will probably need to sing the song several times until everyone has had a turn.
>
>   focus: rolling and trapping

2. ‖   <u>Let's Throw!</u>

      Age: two and a half years and up

      Ratio: open activity

Procedure:

This opportunity can be adapted to provide either simple or complex opportunities, depending on the material that is made available to the children.

You will need a variety of balls and beanbags to throw. Set up a number of situations where the children will be able to throw into, over, or at a target.

Use different size hoops on the floor, different size boxes to throw objects into, and place objects at different heights on the wall as targets. The possibilities are endless.

focus: throwing

3. ‖   <u>"Wall Ball"</u>

      Age: three years and up

      Ratio: open activity

Procedure:

The younger child sits on the floor and rolls the ball to the wall. Older children stand and throw the ball to the wall. They quickly realize that the ball will usually come right back to them.

The "wall" can be used to help with the skills of bouncing, throwing, and catching.

focus: throwing

4. ‖ <u>Kick Ball</u>

Ages: four years and up

Ratio: one to six

Procedure:

The children stand in a circle. There is one ball. The activity is best played in two phases. In the first phase the child moves with the ball as she walks and pushes the ball (dribbles) across the circle to another child. She then changes places with the child she dribbled the ball to. Each child is given an opportunity to push the ball across the circle to another child.

In the second phase the children remain standing in the circle. Rather than dribble the ball, they remain in their places and kick it to someone else around the circle. The game continues until all the children have had an opportunity to kick the ball.

Variation # 1

Age: six years and up

Ratio: one to eight

With schoolage children it is exciting to start the game with one ball and then gradually start to add more balls. Each time you do the activity you might want to challenge the children by adding yet another ball.

Variation # 2

Place an object such as another ball, a bowling pin, or cone in the middle of the circle. Encourage the children to either touch, hit, or knock down the object in the centre with the ball they are kicking.

focus: kicking, dribbling

5. ‖ <u>Scarves</u>

      Age: four to seven years old

      Ratio: one to ten

      Procedure:

Children work on their own to develop and enhance the skill of throwing and catching. Each child is given a scarf to explore. They are encouraged to throw it up in the air and try and catch it before it hits the ground. Educator cues include: "watch it float, catch it on your head, pinch it between your fingers, catch it on your head."

focus: throwing, catching, tactile awareness

6. ‖ <u>Quoits</u>

      Ages: six years and up

      Ratio: open activity

      Procedure:

Children are provided with several rings that look like bracelets. These rings are tossed onto a board with sticks of different heights.

This game is similar to ring toss. You need a good size block or cube with wooden dowels placed upright in it. These dowels should be of varied height and need to be rubber tipped at the top for safety.

Quoits originated in Great Britain. Records indicate that this game seems to have been played at least as early as the fourteenth century.

focus: throwing

REFERENCES

Allen, Eileen K. and Marotz, Lynn (1989) *Developmental Profiles, From Birth to Six.* Albany, New York: Delmar Publishers.

Beaty, Janice J. (1986) *Observing Development of the Young Child.* Columbus, Ohio: Merrill Publishing.

Cratty, Bryant J. (1986) Third edition. *Perceptual and Motor Development in Infants and Children.* Englewood Cliffs, New Jersey.

Gallahue, David L.(b) (1982) *Understanding Motor Development in Children.* New York: John Wiley and Sons.

Gibson, James J. (1966) *The Senses Considered as Perceptual Systems.* Boston: Houghton Mifflin Company.

Grunfeld, Frederic V. (1975) *Games of the World, how to make them, how to play them, how they came to be.* Zurich: Swiss Committee for UNICEF.

Keogh, Jack and Sugden, David (1985) *Movement Skill Development.* New York: MacMillan.

Kirchner, Glenn (1992) 8th edition *Physical Education for Elementary School Children.* Dubuque, Iowa: Wm. C. Brown Publishers.

Laszlo, J.J. and Bairstow, P.J. (1985) *Perceptual-Motor Behaviour, Developmental Assessment and Therapy.* New York: Praeger Publishers.

Lefrancois, Guy R. (1973) *Of Children, An Introduction to Child Development.* Belmont, California: Wadsworth Publishing Company.

Pangrazi, Robert P. & Dauer, Victor P. (1981) *Movement in Early Childhood and Primary Education.* Minneapolis, Minesota: Burgess Publishing Company.

Rosenbaum, David A. (1991) *Human Motor Control.* San Diego: Academic Press Inc.

Trawick-Smith, Jeffrey (1994) *Interactions in the Classroom* New York: MacMillan College Publishing Company.

Wickstrom, Ralph L. (1977) *Fundamental Motor Patterns.* Philadelphia: Lea & Febiger.

Williams, Harriet (1983) *Perceptual and Motor Development.* Enlegwood Cliffs, New Jersey: Prentice-Hall.

Winstein and Schmidt (1989) Second edition. Sensorimotor Feedback, in *Human Skills.* Edited by Holding, London, Great Britain: John Wiley and Sons.

Chapter 7
THE SCHOOLAGE CHILD

In this chapter you will learn about:

- Physical characteristics
    - six to eight years of age
    - nine to eleven years of age
- Attitude and exposure
- Learning Opportunities

THE SCHOOLAGE CHILD

What can the body tell us? Plenty - if we observe how people actually move.

Edward T. Hall

The schoolage years represent a time when boys and girls refine fundamental motor skills and combine them in the pursuit of sport, dance, and everyday living. As general efficiency of movement and cognitive abilities increase, there is greater potential to explore a wide array of sports and organized games. In the later elementary school years, children begin to engage in specialized sports that are of interest to them and that reflect their increased efficiency of movement. Only through repeated opportunity and practice will children be able to actively construct physical knowledge and combine fundamental movement skills.

We will begin our discussion with a look at some of the changing physical characteristics and what impact that has for the educator. We will then discuss attitude and exposure to physical activity. Physical activity is a natural occurrence with infants, toddlers, and preschool children, while the schoolage child does not rely as heavily on movement as a means of exploring the world around. During the schoolage years, physical activity is less readily available as children must sit for many hours of the day and many days of the week behind a desk. Physical movement becomes only one part of the weekly curriculum. All too often it is merely an add-on component.

As the percentage of two-parent working families and single parent families continues to rise, this age group is more often in extended day programming. This chapter primarily focuses on the educator who is predominantly involved with the schoolage child in before and after school programming. The comments and information are however of relevance to anyone involved with this age group.

PHYSICAL CHARACTERISTICS

Six to Eight Years of Age

These are the years when most children are developmentally ready to begin sports that combine and refine fundamental movements. During these years individual growth changes do not seem to be as rapid as they were in infancy (Kirchner, 1992). The differences between boys and girls are minimal but there are marked individual differences in physical size and emotional maturation between children of the same age. Traditionally, this is a time when a child loses baby fat and develops a leaner body and muscular strength improves for both boys and girls. There does not appear to be a great discrepancy in the development of boys and girls at this age. However, on average, boys seem to be slightly taller than girls (Musson, 1994). This is a good age to involve the children in coeducational sports pursuits. Their skill level is relatively well matched and physical activity provides a good forum for learning to work and play together.

You may also find a difference in children's attitude towards physical education based on their cultural orientation and previous exposure. Some cultures look more favourably towards physical education than do others. Some revere individualistic expressions of movement such as tai chi, while others prefer more muscle-bound strength oriented sports such as hockey, boxing, and baseball.

It is important to provide a lot of time for gross motor activity at this age in order to develop heart and lung capacity as well as improve muscle strength and endurance. Materials should be proportional with respect to the size of the children as they are not yet capable of manipulating adult size equipment.

To promote muscle tone and cardiovascular fitness, provide short periods of movement opportunities on a daily basis rather than one or two long periods each week. By short, we mean a minimum of ten minutes. Shorter than this will not give children enough time to get into any game. Use shorter time segments for relaxation activities such as guided fantasies(Chapter 11) or muscle awareness activities such as creative movement (Chapter 11). When active sessions are too short they do not encourage positive development of attention span and problem solving. Children at this stage of development fatigue physically more easily than they do in the years between nine and eleven. It is therefore important to develop stamina by providing frequent opportunities that sustain cardiovascular activity.

Reaction time is another skill that can be developed at this age. Reaction time refers to the interval of time between seeing an object that you have to adjust to, deciding what your reaction should be, then actually responding in the form of an action. As your skill level increases so does your reaction time. For example, in floor hockey, you may not react quickly enough when the oncoming ball is speeding toward you, while at a slower pace, you may experience little difficulty in bringing your stick into the proper place in order to return the puck. As you play hockey more often, your ability to anticipate the ball increases, proportionally reducing reaction time. Reaction time is important in any repetitive tasks, such as those required in most racket sports. Practice helps children learn to anticipate the arrival of a ball. Anticipation reduces reaction time and therefore increases motor output and ultimately sports performance (Holding, 1989). Warmup drills that are lead up activities to the various sports you are involved in are a good way to improve reaction time. It is a good idea to provide games that will help develop reaction time as well. Simple ones include action ball and circle dodge ball, running through obstacles, and games that involve quick changes in direction.

Transference of skill occurs when a child learns one skill and that is then transferred to the performance of another more advanced one. It is effective to introduce a number of *low-level organization* games that will have skills that can be transferred to more advanced games. Let us look at the skill of striking for example. It is fun for children of this age to practise striking by using a long balloon as an implement to strike a round balloon. This activity develops eye-hand coordination. These are the same skills that will later be used in more advanced sports such as badminton or baseball. The balloon swat provides a good opportunity for children to develop movement patterns that will be transferred to sport activity in the later school age years. Low-level organization games are discussed in greater depth in the chapter on nonelimination games. Many low-level organization games that you will introduce should have embedded in their design combinations of skills that are required for more advanced sports pursuits. Avoid drill repetition commonly used in organized elementary physical education sports.

The early school age years are a time when fundamental skills need to be practised to the point where they become automatic. That is to say that the skills become so ingrained that carrying them out is almost routine. Fundamental skills cannot become routine or automatic independently. If this were true, all adults would successfully and accurately throw a ball, dribble a soccer goal, or run with a perfect stride. Early school age years represent an important time for the educator to focus on combining fundamental skills. Many sports require a combination of running, jumping, throwing, and/or striking. For example, in basketball, a person must run, bounce a ball, dodge other people on the court, jump, and throw the ball. In soccer, a person must run, dodge others on the playing field, kick with varying intensity, and kick to a target with accuracy. In tennis, a person must chase, run, stop and start, as well as strike a ball. All these are examples of how sports combine fundamental movement skills.

We have recommended that, in the preschool years, each child have his own ball or equipment in order to establish a sense of continuity and belonging. The concept of sharing is introduced through partner work. Now, during the early school years, young children can benefit from games that require a few children to share equipment. This sharing of equipment provides good lead up to more advanced team sports that require extensive equipment sharing and encourage children to work cooperatively towards a common goal. Target provides a good lead up game to soccer, while Hoops is a good lead up game to basketball.

Nine to Eleven Years of Age

From the age of nine to about eleven, children experience rapid changes in growth and development. Girls on average mature two years ahead of boys physically, reaching puberty during the elementary years (Kirchner, 1992). The majority of boys reach puberty in Secondary I and II. Both sexes are becoming conscious and aware of their bodies. Some children go through this period of transition with ease, while others find themselves self-conscious and shy. There is once again an increase in the rate of individual physical growth (Lefrancois, 1973).

Boys demonstrate a greater mastery of eye-hand coordination at this age. We cannot help but wonder if this is not in large part due to the exposure that boys have to ball sports and to the fact that a parent or some significant other will often come home to play pitch with a son, but how often do you hear about a parent coming home to play pitch with a daughter. Gender biases still exist and we believe they play a part in the marked difference in the development of eye-hand coordination and related skills.

At this stage of development, boys and girls both show a marked increase in physical coordination and have an increased attention span. They are challenged by games that have rules and can follow many rules as well as keep score and referee their own games.

Some children will want to adhere strictly to existing rules while others will be ready and eager to modify rules. You should step in and help children reflect on the situation. Encourage them to decide as a group whether or not to continue the game they are playing with the existing rules or to change them. Changing rules must be a group decision involving conflict resolution to ensure that all children feel the changes are fair. This is an important part of the child's moral and social development because children learn how to resolve conflict fairly and how to identify when their needs are different from others. You can help foster organizational and leadership abilities in children of this age.

Younger schoolage children need an introduction to games with rules, but the rules are usually much less intricate. Discussions can help children make decisions that will impact on their curriculum. By the later school age years, children can and should be given much greater control over their own destiny. They should have a great deal of input into designing their motor curriculum and in selecting the activities and sports that interest them. Let them know that there are times when you will show them a new sport and that this new sport or movement activity can then be added to their curriculum if they choose. Involve the children at all stages of planning. Early arrival or after school, and professional days provide wonderful opportunities for older children to benefit from the responsibility of organizing and leading games for younger children.

Provide longer periods of time for physical activity as both heart and lung capacity are increasing at this age. A ten-minute activity will not sufficiently develop physical and motor fitness. You will need twenty-to-thirty minute blocks of time as a minimum to develop fitness. Longer sport periods also foster increased attention span as children are encouraged to focus on a task. Flitting from sport to class too quickly teaches children to rush.

If you only have ten minutes available, use the time to focus on strength building activities or tension releasers. Teach stretching and physical relaxation skills during the shorter time spans that are available.

In these years it is important to provide children with opportunity to play team games with age appropriate rules. Children should be encouraged to work together within a team. Games like Newcomb Ball and Tenecoit are great at this age.

ATTITUDE AND EXPOSURE

There are many possible opportunities for schoolage children to be exposed to physical activity and sport. This can be part of a physical education program within the school curriculum or part of an extended day program. Children who go home after school can either participate in physical activity outside their front door, in neighbourhood games such as street hockey or hopscotch, and/or they can become involved in structured community and private sport instruction.

Children's attitudes towards sport and physical fitness will influence their desire to participate. Adults need to model a positive attitude towards the pursuit of physical activity if children are to view this part of life favourably. Mind and body must be tuned together for the development of a well rounded person. By the time children reach the schoolage years they should already have developed a good foundation in skill development and positive regard for movement. It is generally in the schoolage years that we find the greatest decline in sports interest. There are numerous factors that play a contributing role. Some include, we believe, a neglect and lack of encouragement from significant adults, a preferential interest in computer and video games, as well as a lack of affordable opportunity for schoolage children to purse sports goals.

Schoolage children love to move and participate vigorously in sport and dance. However, they need the opportunity, positive role models, and a sense that physical activity is valued. Movement needs to be more than just organized sport. It should be incorporated into the daily life. It can happen in the gym, at specialty sports clubs, or in the classroom. It can be vigourous or relaxing. It can be passive or active. It is as important to teach children to move their bodies as it is to teach them to relax their muscles appropriately.

In Canada, there is a difference in the amount of time devoted to physical education within each province. A Gallup poll was commissioned by the Canadian Association for Health, Physical Education and Recreation (CAHPER) in 1991 to determine where our elementary school children are in terms of their exposure to physical education. A wide discrepancy was found from province to province. Alberta elementary schools offer 90 minutes per week of physical education while Saskatchewan schools fared better offering 150 minutes per week. Various school boards offer only a single physical education class per week. "The province of Quebec stands out in this study for having the lowest levels of daily physical education, the lowest incidence of intramural activities and the lowest incidence of interscholastic athletic programs" (CAPHER). In contrast to Quebec, its neighbour Ontario seemed to fair best, having on average a large number of schools in the system offering daily physical activity sessions.

Grades 1 and 2 are critical years in attitude development towards physical activity and sport. These are years when children can be easily turned on to or off of physical activity. Successful mastery of skills will lead to positive self-esteem, which is necessary to increase the desire to continue the pursuit of physical activity.

The following anecdote provides an example of how children can be encouraged to pursue a motor task without pressure. In the situation described below, Jessie needed to develop her coordination and balance. The educator provided ample time and praise in order to help Jessie achieve motor success.

◆ ◆ ◆

Jessie, in Grade 1, was learning to jump rope. She tried over and over again to judge the timing of the rope as it was brought around, and adjust her jump accordingly. She tried shortening and lengthening the rope until the task seemed to work. Determination led to motor success. Proud of her new achievement, she would jump rope at every chance.

◆ ◆

Not all children have the same degree of difficulty in refining motor skills. Some may find they have perceptual and motor skills that easily transfer from a previously learned experience to the new task, such as jumping rope. Some children have good ability to throw and catch. They quickly and easily transfer this fundamental skill to ball games such as soccer, baseball, or tennis, while others have greater difficulty refining fundamental skills for sports use. Another example is the varying degree of refinement that a schoolage child demonstrates in fine motor tasks. Some children easily move from beading to knitting and sewing, while others find this much more challenging. You can be of the greatest assistance by providing enough time for children to practise refinement of motor skills and by positively encouraging children in order to help them pursue their goals.

At about age ten, there seems to be a marked change in physical development. The schoolager becomes stronger and has greater perceptual and cognitive skills. This leads to better coordination, especially with respect to eye-hand coordination. This translates to the ability to be physically capable in many sports. Cognitive development contributes to a superior ability to interpret information such as the speed of an incoming ball, or how to adjust one's body in order to react to an object or a teammate in a game situation. These skills increase to a greater extent in the years from nine to eleven than they did from six to eight.

In general, there is a better understanding of rules when playing games. It becomes appropriate to introduce games that require a higher degree of organization. Sports with increased attention to perceptual motor skills are appropriate. For example, tennis is a sport that requires advanced perceptual and eye-hand coordination skills. On the other hand, gymnastics relies to a greater extent on the use of body coordination.

The following anecdote provides an interesting example of the use of cognitive and perceptual information by a nine-year-old child learning to play tennis.

♦ ♦ ♦

Lauren, age nine, began taking tennis lessons. She played for two months and experienced frustration when her timing was off. She could see the ball coming, would swing her racket and miss the ball regularly. After about two months she switched the racket from her right hand to her left hand and became much more successful at hitting the ball. This to her was a revelation as she said: "I can hit much better with my left hand." By the way, Lauren is left-handed.

♦ ♦

Lauren was given the chance to problem solve and determine for herself how to improve her coordination in the game of tennis. At first she modelled what the instructor and other children did. Whether playing with her right or left hand, her eye-hand skills and perceptual skills were the same. Coordination was different. The instructor provided a positive learning environment where Lauren had a chance to experiment on her own without the fear of competition. She was given the time to problem solve that ultimately led to motor success. Although two months may seem to some like a long time to let a child use the wrong hand, we do not see this as an issue at such a young age. Keep children interested at all costs! This is the key to a successful school age motor program.

CHAPTER HIGHLIGHTS

It is important to ensure that children practise fundamental movement skills in order for them to become automatic. This helps achieve success in combining and refining them for the purpose of sports and games. *What does it mean when a skill is automatic?* Well, think of the motor instructions you give yourself when walking or sitting. You don't think about it. You just do it. We don't concentrate on putting one foot in front of the other nor do we check the height of a seat before sitting down. An automatic skill is one we no longer think through.

Sports games take fundamental motor skills and combine them in a variety of ways. This mixing of skills adds complexity to motor output. It is important to combine them sequentially from simple to complex. What this means is that first you need to observe the children and assess what level they are at in motor ability. This will change slightly each year within the same age group. In Grades 1 and 2 you might introduce the game of Target as a lead up to soccer. In this game children combine the skills of kicking and trapping, both necessary for soccer. The game is only introduced when successful combinations of the necessary skills are achieved. Use your own ideas to supplement any other steps that are needed before actually introducing the game. It is important that you "gradually increase the complexity of tasks" and "consider the sequence of activities at all instructional levels"(Peterson, JOPERD, 1992, p.26).

Physical education opportunities in the schoolage years should provide a balance between games of low-level organization and simple team games and work towards games with a higher degree of organization and skill. There should be a combination of open ended activities designed for self-selection and structured games that may have greater educator input. We caution the educator to strive for a minimum of intervention. Striking a balance through programming is explored further throughout the next section of this book.

LEARNING OPPORTUNITIES

1. ‖   Target

Age: six years and up

Ratio: partner activity

Procedure:

Organize children into pairs and give each pair one ball. Draw two lines across the room. Initially these lines can be closer together, about five feet (1.5 metres). They can be placed farther apart as the children's proficiency level increases. One partner from the pair should stand behind one line facing his partner who is standing behind the other line. The object of the game is for one partner to kick the ball from behind his line. The ball cannot be thrown, only kicked. The other partner must catch the ball with his hands without crossing the line. The children then reverse roles. The game should continue as long as it is interesting.

X   O

X   O

focus: catching, kicking, balance

2. ‖   <u>Hoops</u>

> **Age:**   six years and up
>
> **Ratio:**   partner activity
>
> **Procedure:**

Divide the class into pairs and give each a ball. Two or three lowered basketball nets or hoops, placed between two chairs, are located at either end of the playing area. The object of the game is to get the ball into at least one basket on either side of the room. Children may move forward by dribbling the ball up to three times, then they must throw it to their partner who can dribble the ball for up to three times. When a member of the pair is close to a hoop he tries to sink a basket. Each team keeps track of how many baskets they score.

focus: throwing, bouncing, dribbling, catching, locomotor movements

3. ‖   <u>Circle Avoid Ball</u>

> **Age:**   six years and up
>
> **Ratio:**   one to twelve
>
> **Procedure:**

Have children form a circle with one child standing in the centre. We recommend that circles be kept to a maximum of ten or twelve children. If the group is too large, use two circles. The object of this game is for the child(ren) inside the circle to avoid the ball as members of the circle try to tap them with the ball. Once hit, the person in the circle joins the perimeter and another child goes into the centre.*

focus: throwing, catching, physical fitness, locomotor skills

*Note: We recommend you use a bouncy sponge ball and insist that hits must be below the waist. This will focus on the skills of dodging and throwing while avoiding potential injury.

4. ‖ <u>Potato Sack Hop</u>

    Age: seven years and up

    Ratio: one to ten

    Procedure:

Each child is given a large potato sack to climb into. He pulls it up to the waist and hops around the room. A start and finish point can be assigned to add a challenge. (Old pillowcases make good sacks.)

focus: jumping, hopping, physical fitness, balance

5. ‖ <u>Newcomb Ball</u>

    Age: nine years and up

    Ratio: one to twelve

    Procedure:

A great lead up game to volleyball. Setup involves a badminton net and a ball. Six children are on either side of the net. The object of the game is to keep the ball in play. Each time a team drops a ball, their opponent gets a point. Ball is set into play by tossing it over the net. A child on the opposing team must catch it and toss it to two other members on his team. The third person to catch the ball must send it back over the net. The procedure is repeated. Game continues until one team has six points. Then teams should be reorganized. As children become more proficient, raise the height of the net to provide greater challenge.

focus: throwing, catching, eye-hand coordination, teamwork

6. ‖   <u>Tenecoit</u>

> **Age:**   nine years and up
>
> **Ratio:**   one to twelve
>
> **Procedure:**
>
> This is played with exactly the same rules as "Newcomb Ball" except that a round rubber floor hockey ring is used instead. The ring must be caught above the elbow.
>
> focus: eye-hand coordination, grasping, reaching, throwing, spatial awareness, visual awareness

Photo 7.1. Lead up activity to the game of tenecoit.

REFERENCES

CAHPER (1991) *Canadian Association for Health, Physical Education and Recreation*, Ottawa, Ontario.

Hall, Edward T. (1981) *Beyond Culture.* New York: Doubleday, Anchor Books.

Holding, Dennis H. (1989) "Skills Research" in *Human Skills*. Second edition. Chichester, New York: John Wiley and Sons.

Kirchner, Glenn (1992) *Physical Education for Elementary School Children*. Dubuque: Iowa. Wm. C. Brown Publishers.

Lefrancois, Guy R. (1973) *Of Children, An Introduction to Child Development*. Belmont: California. Wadsworth Publishing.

Musson, Steve (1994) *School-Age Care, Theory and Practice*. Don Mills, Ontario: Addison-Wesley.

Peterson, Susan C. "The Sequence of Instruction in Games: Implications for Developmentally Appropriateness, *Journal Of Physical Education, Recreation and Dance*, Reston: Virginia, AAPHER, August, 1992, Vol. 63, No. 6, pp. 36-43.

Weiller, Karen H. "The Social-Emotional Components of Physical Education for Children, *Journal of Physical Education, Recreation and Dance*, Aug., 1992, Vol. 63, No. 6, pp.50-56.

PART III

WHAT NOW?

In this chapter you will learn about:

- Factors that influence planning
- Observations
- Developmentally appropriate planning
- Environment
  - preschool
  - schoolage
  - outdoor
- Equipment
- Selection of learning opportunities
- Learning Opportunities

PLANNING

Education has to focus on each child - not each child considered in isolation but each child seen in relation with the other children....with the environment of the school, with the community, with the wider society.... To know how to plan and proceed with their work, teachers listen to and observe children carefully.

Lella Gandini

Now, more than ever, it is important to ensure that children have ample time and opportunity to become involved in movement experiences. All too often these activities take a back seat in our present world of technology. With television, video games, and computers competing for time, the importance of planning and including movement opportunities into the daily program cannot be underestimated. According to Nash (1989, p.143), "It is easier for a child to reflect on physical prowess than on growing mental abilities. For this reason the gross motor component of any program is an important one."

Our aim for this section of the book is to pull together those features which enhance and develop gross and fine motor development, perceptual motor development, physical fitness, and balance. We include such topics as nonelimination games, the parachute, and creative movement. These are areas where we have had enjoyment and success with the children. We are confident that these ideas will point you in the right direction when confronted with the task of planning and preparing a developmentally appropriate program.

FACTORS THAT INFLUENCE PLANNING

There are many important and crucial factors that influence how, when, what, and where you will plan your movement opportunities. One of the most significant factors is your view of how children learn. Our concepts regarding how children learn have been discussed throughout the book. In general, we believe that children learn through a variety of situations and that not all children learn in the same way or at the same rate. They learn from both teacher directed activities, open-ended activities, and from spontaneous experiences. Bredekamp and Rosegrant (1992) view the role of the educator as providing and supporting guidance and facilitating children's development and learning. They also believe that children learn in a circular fashion, beginning with an awareness of a situation or an object and followed by exploration, which then leads to inquiry and utilization of the object.

Other significant factors that influence programming include available resources both in terms of the environment and equipment, ages of the children, size of the group, adult-child ratio, as well as the season of the year, and cultural limitations. This chapter addresses each of these factors and provides a framework from which to develop and design your own program. We do not attempt to lay out a specific curriculum as the many variables that exist within each program would make the task impossible. Rather, we will provide you with the ingredients to consider and a curriculum framework to input your ideas and those elements that need to be included in your program in order to develop one that reflects the uniqueness of your centre and children.

OBSERVATIONS

Effective planning requires observations. The importance of observations and methods of observations were discussed in Chapter 1. We have previously highlighted the importance of allocating sufficient time for observations and how to best use the checklists. Checklists have been included in several chapters to facilitate the process of observation. They will give you an overall indication of what level each child is at. Planning will reflect the results of these observations.

Once you have completed your observations it is a good idea to set some goals or objectives. Knowing where you are going helps to create a positive learning environment. The types of opportunities you plan should be designed from simple to complex and should reflect both the children's interests and their level of competency. Important questions to ask yourself include: *What do the children like to do? What are they able to do?* It is essential to provide children with opportunities that offer enjoyment, meet their needs, and provide that extra challenge. This approach to planning is critical and will allow for a developmentally appropriate program.

DEVELOPMENTALLY APPROPRIATE PROGRAMMING

Designing and planning a developmentally appropriate program is both an interesting and challenging task. Developmentally appropriate practice "is a framework, a philosophy, or an approach to working with young children that requires the adult pay attention to at least two important pieces of information -- what we know about how children develop and learn and what we learn about the individual needs and interests of each child in the group" (Bredekamp and Rosegrant, 1992, p.4). The traditional obstacle course provides an excellent example to illustrate this approach. A traditional obstacle course would have a variety of equipment and material set out for children to climb, crawl through, or hop over. Children are expected to follow the course and they are each allowed to have a turn. Often children spend a long time waiting for their turn. In some situations we have observed that children will wait as much as six to eight minutes for a turn and then when they finally do the obstacle course, they complete it within three to four minutes. A tremendous amount of time is spent waiting with a minimal amount of time spent actively involved.

Another problem that occurs with this traditional design of an obstacle course is that children complete the tasks required with limited encouragement to explore the equipment. They graze through the apparatus quickly rather than spending sufficient time in any one area. This limits potential development and enhancement of skills. It also reduces problem solving experiences by limiting time to find solutions in terms of ways to go over, under, or through a piece of equipment. In the traditional obstacle course children are more concerned with finishing, rather than finding out more about what their bodies are capable of.

A more appropriate approach to the traditional obstacle course is to eliminate the notion of a "course." Eliminate the concept of a place to start and a place to finish. We find that permitting open exploration of each piece of equipment in any order can allow for increased attention span and a greater opportunity to practise skills. The children also have the freedom to move from area to area when they are ready. If one part of your setup becomes too crowded, simply redirect some of the children to another apparatus until there is space available. Point out to them that the large number of children poses a safety issue. Never redirect without giving a valid rationale. In this way all the children are actively exploring at all times and are afforded the respect and courtesy they deserve.

The type of program you design will vary depending on whether you are in a half day or a full day program. Regardless of the variables, we believe that you should provide a combination of open-ended and teacher directed activities. Within both open-ended and teacher directed activities attention needs to be given to individual and group experiences. Individualized opportunities need to be child initiated and self-directed ones that allow each child to work at her own level and pace. Each child must also be able to try things in new ways. The outcome is not a product or specific skill success. Rather, it is the pleasure of exploration and the learning that comes from deciding how to do something. Letting the children try things in their own way permits them to figure out the equipment, problem solve, and in most situations it enables them to be creative. Creative movement and guided opportunities provide a perfect time to meet individual needs. They give the children the possibility to explore and manipulate materials and equipment at their own level and in their own way.

In group situations, as with many other situations, there is more than just the initial focus. You may be working with a group and have gross motor abilities as your primary focus. If you set up the activities appropriately an important secondary focus of enhancing social skills evolves. Being part of a group permits each child to see how other children tackle a situation. It helps them recognize individual strength in others. The individual strengths can then be combined to make the group's opportunity a successful and challenging experience. The parachute and cooperative games provide excellent opportunities for the group to work together.

Ensure that there is a balance and blend of locomotor, nonlocomotor, and manipulative activities. Flexibility and choice are the key to a developmentally appropriate program and will enable you to meet the needs of the children and provide a stimulating challenge as well. Appendix A provides some interesting examples and clarification on developmentally appropriate physical education for children.

THE ENVIRONMENT

Use your environment to its maximum potential. Sometimes movement experiences need to be quiet and solitary. At other times, it is wise to involve children in group experiences that are more active in nature. Your decision will be influenced by your goals and objectives. *Are you trying to create a calming effect, rev up energy, or develop fitness?*

We have broken down the discussion of the environment into three sections: 1) preschool, 2) schoolage, and 3) the outdoor environment.

Preschool Environment

Educators in nursery schools and day cares have a variety of environments to deal with, resulting in many challenges to overcome in order to provide a developmentally appropriate program. This is where you can rely on your creative skills, resourcefulness, and flexibility in planning and organizing your environment. "Modern approaches to motor education recognize the influence of both environment and maturation" (Trawick-Smith, p. 270). Generate the most out of what you have!

Some centres are fortunate to have a separate room designed and designated for gross motor activity. Other centres have the educators convert their classroom space to allow for gross motor opportunities. If you are in a centre where there is limited space available for gross motor opportunities, you might want to consider finding additional space in the community that could be used once or twice a week for this purpose. Church basements, synagogue facilities, community centres, or park chalets are only a few of the many facilities that could be explored.

Regardless, there are many different ways in which the design and setup can be created to ensure that movement opportunities are incorporated into the program. Should you predominantly use your classroom space for gross motor opportunities, you might want to consider team teaching for these periods of the day. In many centres, educators use this time of the day to team up and work with other educators who have children of similar ages. For example, while you set up and organize the material and equipment for the gross motor opportunity, your fellow educator can be close by with the children, singing songs or preparing them for the activities.

Incorporating motor equipment during free play is an extremely valuable venue in planning for group and individual needs. Often the type of material we choose to set out during free play will allow the children to practise their skills independently. Use furniture to help create challenging and interesting spaces. A row of chairs can make a great tunnel for crawling through.

Activities set out during free play allow the children to work at their own pace and set their own challenges. The following anecdote is an example of a child testing his own limits through play prompted by the educator's choice of materials.

♦ ♦ ♦

> *Michael went over to the carpet area and picked up the beanbags positioned near some cardboard boxes. At first he stood very close to the box and was able to throw them all in. He then took a few steps back and started all over. Again he was successful. He then moved over to the next box, which was designed with a smaller box inside the larger one. Michael started to throw the beanbags and was successful about 50 percent of the time. He then moved in closer to the box to try again until he was able to reach the target each time.*

♦ ♦

The above example demonstrates how simple cardboard boxes and a few beanbags can supply inexpensive, challenging motor exploration. Table 8.1. offers some examples of materials that can be used during free play.

SET UP MATERIALS FOR SELF SELECTION		
FREE PLAY		
LOCOMOTOR	**BALANCE**	**MANIPULATION**
climbing frame	rocking boat	beanbags
slide	stilts	basketball net
horizontal ladders	balance beam	streamers
wedged mats	balance board	scarves
ROTATE AND VARY MATERIALS ON A REGULAR BASIS		

TABLE 8.1. Set up of materials for self selection

Schoolage Environment

The environment of the schoolage care program often differs from that of the preschool child. Often these programs can be located in or close to community facilities that have built-in resources or in elementary schools where a gymnasium is usually available.

Firstly, you should establish what opportunities exist and are available to you before you begin to design your program. For example, one option might be to use the swimming pool in the fall and spring and use the arena during the winter. The type of activities that you provide during the year should be varied. Secondly, you might assess what physical experiences are available to the children during the day. In the school environment you might coordinate the motor program between the extended day educator and the regular teacher. For example, if there is a high degree of cooperative games during the day, you could include individual pursuits or team sports during the afterschool program.

Many sports activities require safety equipment. As an educator it is important that you ensure there is adequate provision of such equipment and, if you are engaging in the sport with the children, model appropriate behaviour and wear the protective garb. The key is to strike a balance in planning an overall curriculum by communicating with all those individuals in your school who provide any part of the physical education program.

Outdoor Environment

The outdoor environment provides another avenue to promote and develop gross and fine motor development. Outdoor play environments come in a variety of designs and functions. "Special consideration should be given to making playscapes magical, enchanting places. These special touches are intended to transform mundane, over-slick, sterile playgrounds into places that invite, challenge, and satisfy -- places that transcend the ordinary and allow children to create, wonder and, consequently, to grow" (Frost, 1992, p.157).

The most convenient outdoor environment is the area right outside your centre. In general most outdoor areas have some type of permanent play structure as well as portable outdoor equipment. Having portable equipment that can enhance and stimulate a variety of play situations is extremely valuable. Outdoor play environments should also include plans for a variety of experiences. This planning can be approached in several ways. For example, some centres divide their planning into morning and afternoon sessions. The morning is left for free choice of the permanent outdoor equipment and the afternoon is the time when alternate equipment, such as the parachute or balls, are provided. This order can easily be reversed. Other centres rotate the responsibility for planning for outdoor time on either a daily or weekly basis.

Your outdoor environment also includes those areas available in your community. Community parks and indoor recreational facilities are important facilities to recruit, as many include a swimming pool and/or an arena. A "Y" facility as well as an elementary school will include a gym.

Before taking a group of children to the park it is a good idea to visit the park ahead of time to check for both safety concerns and appropriateness for the group of children that you are working with. There may be times when the park that is the most convenient may not be the most appropriate for your age group of children. It is important to then try and find alternate facilities. As previously indicated generate the most out of what you have! Maximize these areas to their fullest potential.

EQUIPMENT

Think of your room as a large empty space that you can divide and fill in whatever way meets the needs and provides the appropriate challenges for the children. For example, if your focus is on throwing and tossing you would set out space reflecting these skills. You could decide to put out a basketball net and a large bin in which to throw the balls. This area could also have at least three types of balls (such as rubber, foam, or plastic) of varying sizes. As mentioned in Chapter 6 children learn first to throw a small ball and then move on to larger ones. Consequently, this particular area should provide many levels of difficulty where the children could self-select any or all of the three balls. This is an example of how one of many areas could be set up for a guided opportunity related to throwing and tossing. The age and size of the group will dictate your choice in the amount and type of areas that you set up. The possibilities for setup and design of your gross motor spaces are endless. We encourage you to be both creative and innovative and use materials and equipment in novel ways.

As with the environment, use your creative skills to provide variety in the type of equipment you can make available. Exchanging and sharing equipment in the centre and in the school environment adds variability. You will often need to improvise. For example, if you are working on balance and you do not have a balance beam you might want to consider using a bench. At first the bench can be used just to walk across, but as the children's skills improve the bench can be turned over. The bottom of a bench is usually supported by a narrower strip of wood, which makes an excellent balance beam.

♦ ♦ ♦

In a recent observation a bench was put out during free play for the children to practise walking across, to increase their balance. However, one child decided to climb up and jump off onto the mats below. This action interested, the other children enticing the whole group to take turns climbing and jumping off the bench.

♦ ♦

This simple opportunity, selected by the educator and based on the available materials, provided the children with the means to create their own play and fostered balance, locomotion, and cooperation.

There are numerous ways to create and design tunnels. Putting blankets over small tables or chairs or putting mats over two benches are but a few ideas. Many opportunities for tossing and throwing can also be created with homemade or recycled pieces of material. For example, in some bookstores you will find cardboard stands that display their most current paperback bestsellers. These pieces make great targets to toss into. Involve parents in helping you to design and construct other pieces of equipment. Have them sew beanbags and then have the children help you fill the bags. This allows them to become involved as well.

SELECTION OF LEARNING OPPORTUNITIES

"Movement is a viable and important part of the daily curriculum - not an add-on". (Taylor, 1991, p.143). All too often some educators feel that motor tasks are accomplished for the day because they have led a finger play or movement song. We recognize and believe in the value and potential of such experiences, but they are not a substitute for a comprehensive motor program. Planned experiences, daily routines, self-selected motor play, are all an integral part of the motor curriculum. "In the developmental scheme of things, the focus is truly on the large motor skills for preschool children. It is the foundation for much of the rest of the child's development to follow. Parents and teachers alike want the foundation to be a strong one" (Beaty, 1992, p.270).

We all work hard at planning. We try to present children with opportunities that are enjoyable and that will enhance their skills. Sometimes the best laid plans do not always work. Be flexible and sometimes spontaneous. In a recent experience with the parachute the importance of flexibility was put to the test.

♦ ♦ ♦

> *The children were sitting on the floor shaking the parachute. One child decided to go under the parachute. It didn't take long before several more children wanted to go under as well. Hiding under the parachute was not one of the planned opportunities. However, given the interest of the children the activity was changed to incorporate the notion of hiding under the parachute. The gross motor activity quickly changed into a game of memory where the children had to cover their eyes and guess who was hiding under the parachute.*

♦ ♦

The intended piece of equipment, the parachute, was still being used, and so were the ideas of the children. Their needs and the parachute were incorporated into one. It is important to remember that how one group of children approaches an opportunity is usually very different from the way other groups will approach the same opportunity. One group of children could spend twenty minutes playing Alligator while another group could lose interest after five minutes. *What do you do then?* Try a variation of the game or move on to the next one that you planned to do.

How you pace your movement opportunities is also crucial. You need to pace yourself and the children. Our experience has helped us acquire the knowledge that over-planning, or having more ideas and activities than you need seems to be the key to success. We would recommend a warmup time. Several of the learning opportunities throughout this book could be used as warmup opportunities. The learning opportunities at the end of the chapter will also include several suggestions. The warm-up is usually a quick easy-to-follow opportunity that sets the tone and involves all the children. It is usually active rather than passive. This is then followed by group opportunities or guided opportunities. The session is then concluded with a cooldown. A guided fantasy is one unique and creative way to end a session, allowing the children to relax and use their imagination. An example of a guided fantasy as well as several other cooldown opportunities are included at the end of the chapter. In general, the cooldown is more passive, involves the whole group, and is generally led by the facilitator.

It brings you, the educator, back into a leadership role so that you can direct the group to the next part of the day.

CHAPTER HIGHLIGHTS

The discussion in this chapter provides a framework from which you can design and develop your own movement program. The numerous variables, environment, equipment, age of the children, size of the group, time of year, that influence and impact on the design and implementation of the program have been discussed. The needs of both the individual as well as those of the group must be met. Ensure that there is a combination of opportunities and designs within the program.

In closing, we ask you to challenge yourself to design a developmentally appropriate and diverse curriculum that will best meet the needs of the children with whom you are working.

LEARNING OPPORTUNITIES

1. <u>Hello Song</u>

     Age: three years and up

     Ratio: three to five years, one to eight
                   six to eight years, one to twelve

Procedure:

This is an echo song. As the children gather together you have them sit in a circle. Tell the children that you are going to help them learn a new song, and that they will need to repeat the words after you.

Verse # 1

Educator : HEL LO , there is an accent on each syllable separately. The educator slaps one knee for "Hel" and the other knee for "Lo."
Children: The children repeat the HEL LO and slap their knees.

This is repeated three times by the educator and the children respond three times.

Verse # 2

Educator: GOOD NESS IT'S GOOD TO SEE YOU TO DAY. Each syllable is articulated. On each syllable the educator slaps the floor to create a sound to go with each syllable.
Children: The children repeat GOOD NESS IT'S GOOD TO SEE YOU TO DAY, and they slap the floor as well.

This is repeated three times as well.

Verse # 3

Educator: GOOD BYE and waves good-bye.
Children: The children repeat GOOD BYE and wave goodbye.

This is repeated three times.

Variation # 1

The actions for each of the sections can be changed to suit your group. You could have the children stand for the song. Instead of slapping the knees and the floor, they stamp their feet on each syllable. You could even have actions that have you and the children move while saying the words to the song. Make up actions to go with the beat as you repeat the syllables.(from workshop with Joyce Boorman: University of Alberta, Edmonton: Alberta.)

focus: auditory perception, body awareness, nonlocomotor

2. ‖ <u>Shake Your Sillies Out</u>

    Age: three to six years

    Ratio: one to ten

    Procedure:

Either sing the verse while you and the children shake your body all over any way you want to or sing with Raffi music in the background. See Raffi record <u>More Singable Songs</u> (1977), catalogue number CTR-004.

focus: auditory perception, body awareness, nonlocomotor, locomotor

3. ‖   <u>Up Goes the Castle</u>

    Age: all

    Ratio: will vary depending on the age of the children

    Procedure:

    Children lie flat on their backs. They may close their eyes if they are comfortable but it is not necessary. Each child is given a small ball to hold. Ask them to place the ball on their stomach. As they take a deep breath in tell them to concentrate on their ball. Is it moving? Does it go up or down? What happens when you breath out? Play soothing music in the background to set the mood.

    focus: auditory perception, body awareness

REFERENCES

Beaty, Janice J. (1992) *Preschool Appropriate Practice.* Fort Worth: Harcourt Brace Jovanovich College Publishers.

Bredekamp, Sue & Rosegrant, Teresa editors (1992) *Reaching Potentials: Appropriate Curriculum and Assessment for Young Children.* Vol. 1. Washington: National Association For Education Of Young Children.

Frost, Joe L. (1992) *Play and Playscapes.* Albany, New York: Delmar Publishers.

McKay, Donald, Mitchell, Wendy, Flemming, Bonnie M., Hamilton Softely, Darlene, & Deal Hicks, Joanne (1993) *Creative Teaching in Early Childhood Education*, 2nd edition. Toronto: Harcourt, Brace.

Nash, Chris (1989) *The Learning Environment*, 2nd edition. Toronto: Canada: Collier Macmillan.

Sanders, Stephen (1992) *Designing Preschool Movement Programs.* Champaign, Il: Human Kinetics Books.

Sullivan, Molly (1982) *Feeling Strong, Feeling Free: Movement Exploration for Young Children.* Washington: NAEYC.

Trawick-Smith, Jeffrey (1994) *Interaction in the Classroom.* New York: Macmillan College Publishing.

Taylor, Barbara J. (1991) *A Child Goes Forth*, 7th edition. New York: Macmillan Publishing Company.

In this chapter you will learn about:

- Nonelimination games
    - individual experiences
    - partner experiences
    - group experiences
- Cooperative games
    - identifying cooperative games
    - the benefits of cooperative games
- Competitive games using a nonelimination format
    - playing as a team
- Learning opportunities

NONELIMINATION GAMES

Development of play skills are best fostered through experiences that provide children with many opportunities to practice skills as well as to compare and contrast their ideas with others. Nonelimination games give teachers a structure for organized play that provides maximum skill development time through participatory play.

Barbara Marcus

The focus of this chapter is on *nonelimination games*. We define nonelimination games as those activities, opportunities, and games that require total group participation. All members of the group can participate simultaneously on an individual level, with partners or in groups. Nonelimination games provide the greatest opportunity for motor development as there is a maximum of playing time. Compare this to elimination games where playing time can be limited as a result of a player being "out" for any length of time. When a player is "out" the game is over for them and the remainder of the time is spent watching rather than doing. This often leads to frustration, adds unnecessary stress to the young child's life, and reduces the amount of time the player spends participating and learning through hands-on experience. Through whole group involvement, players can develop personal, cooperative and/or competitive skills.

The word *games* means many things to many people. Our discussion will be limited to games with movement oriented components. We will present a variety of games ranging from those with fewer and simpler rules to those with greater numbers and more elaborate rules. Games with limited rules will be referred to as *low organizational games.*

Usually the nonelimination team games will rely on an outsider such as a referee to regulate the play and ensure that the rules are followed. Games such as volleyball or tennis are more easily self-regulated, while games with larger action components, such as hockey or soccer, require the perspective of an outsider to regulate the play. Games are enjoyed by children of all ages and come in a variety of designs and formats. "Games have good recreational value, provide opportunity for fitness and offer a necessary outlet for natural exuberance." (Pangrazi and Dauer, 1981, p.254). Depending on the organization and framework of a game, it can have either a positive or negative effect on children's prosocial behaviour(Grineski, 1989).

Cooperative and competitive forms of nonelimination games have a purpose in our society and serve to meet the needs of developing children. Cooperative games are developmentally appropriate for both preschool and school age children, whereas nonelimination competitive games are cognitively appropriate for school age children. Both include the social skills of working together and practising the art of negotiation. There is no exclusion, so all participants play as long as they are interested. No one has to wait around for a turn. Parachute play adapts itself to inclusion of the group rather than exclusion of any player. It has so many other unique components that we felt it necessary to devote an entire chapter (Chapter 10) to this piece of equipment.

The first part of this chapter will focus on the players' perspective, looking at individual experiences to partner and group interactions. We will then look at cooperative games and how to identify them and their benefits, and finally at competitive games and the value of team play. In both cooperative and competitive games we will examine the effective involvement of cooperative skills, the importance of these movement games, and their place in the overall curriculum. This chapter will have greater relevance to those working with young children who have acquired a basic mastery of the fundamental motor skills. A good movement curriculum will provide a variety of games and individual opportunities for success.

INDIVIDUAL EXPERIENCES

There are many activities and opportunities where the whole class participates but the games are neither cooperative nor competitive in nature. Although the children all participate at the same time, they work independently and in their own personal space. Games like Sally Says and creative movement opportunities present a few examples of this. In Sally Says, each child tries to carry out the action that is called out. When an error is made, it is identified, and the child continues to participate in the game. Each child is simply exploring movements independently, without the threat or embarrassment of being eliminated. In Sally Says, there is a correct and incorrect response, but an incorrect response is treated lightly and does not reduce anyone's playing time.

In creative movement opportunities, which are explored in detail later in this book, we see individual experiences, which, like Sally Says, involve whole group participation. The difference is that in creative movement there is no correct or incorrect response. Each individual works towards personal goals and is encouraged to explore his own movement potential.

PARTNER EXPERIENCES

Partner experiences provide the simplest level of group games and represent one of the first ways that children learn to work together in organized activity or game situations. "Early emphasis should be on learning to play well together" (Pangrazi and Dauer, 1981, p.255). Partner activities generally require fewer rules and as such are recognized as having a low-level organizational framework. Partner activities can be as rudimentary as one child rolling a ball to another or as interdependent as *partner head and shoulders* (see learning opportunities). Partner experiences can be serious or hilarious, depending on the instructions and rules. An examples such as Mirroring tends to be carried out more seriously, while Partner Pull-up always gets a good laugh. Select learning opportunities that will set the tone or mood you are looking for as well as those that will provide the skill development that you are interested in working on. Initially partner experiences are cooperative in nature. As children reach the later school age years, many partner games can be successfully played in a competitive form. This will be addressed later on in the chapter under the heading of "Competitive Games".

Rules can sometimes pose problems for younger children. They interpret them at their level of understanding, which may be different from that of the educator's perspective. Young children sometimes change the rules as they go along. At three and four years of age, children are primarily interested in what they are doing. They are not interested nor do they think about comparing their performance with that of someone else (Kamii and DeVries, 1980). Around the age of five or six there is a shift in the way children interact in their activities. Things are no longer centred totally around themselves, there is less egocentricity. Children "begin to compare performances and coordinate players' intentions. Without this comparison and coordination, there can be no game" (Kamii and DeVries, 1980, p.24). As cognitive and socioaffective abilities increase, more complex forms of activities can be successfully accomplished and children can follow more instructions of increasing complexity.

GROUP EXPERIENCES

In group experiences, three or more children interact. Often group games involve the whole class working together. Group experiences provide an excellent opportunity to develop interpersonal skills. Children must cooperate for play to be effective. Sometimes this involves negotiating skills or the art of compromise. Group games can also involve low level organization or be more complex in nature. In the preschool years we recommend lower level organization. In the school age years, more complex rules can and should be included. In the school age years, group experiences often involve team play, with one group playing against another. We will see in our discussion of cooperative games that this can mean working to achieve one goal, or in our discussion of competitive games different players can have opposing goals.

When organizing children into two or more groups, we suggest that they be matched according to ability to ensure that groups are balanced. Matching according to ability does not mean that only good players are paired together and weaker players together. It means that there is diversity within each group but the overall picture reflects equilibrium.

COOPERATIVE GAMES

Identifying Cooperative Games

Cooperative games or activities can involve either a pair of children or a group of children. How do you recognize if a game is cooperative? There are five main criteria to look for.
1. There is potential for the whole group to participate.
2. All players work towards a common goal or end result. This criterion must be met if the game is indeed cooperative.
3. There is no elimination process and all children participate throughout the play.
4. The design of the game does not foster competition between the players.
5. There are no winners and no losers.

Cooperative games are designed for whole group participation. However, children should be given the choice to enter or not enter the game situation. Sometimes they are tired and prefer to play alone in a quiet area of the room. There should be some provision for such options, but the game design must have room for all players.

In cooperative games the children are all working toward one common goal. As children play and move together there is opportunity to refine fundamental motor skills and help them develop from an initial stage to a more mature stage. When effectively introduced to a group, cooperative games can teach children to empathize with each other as they must try to see each others perspective. They learn to get along because the game is only successful through mutual agreement and compromise. The children must learn to work in a positive environment in order to ensure the game's success and of course, all this will ultimately serve to bring the group closer together. The level of social cooperation already existing within the group is an important consideration in planning. Children must be cognitively ready to compromise for this type of game to work. We use parachute games and simple partner activities in the preschool years, reserving more advanced cooperative games for the school age years.

Circle Untangle, described in the Learning Opportunity section, provides an excellent example of whole group cooperation. Each member of the group tries to achieve the common goal of forming. Players must all must continue to hold hands throughout. In Circle Untangle, it is the success of the group effort that is important.

Photo 9.1. Circle Untangle

In cooperative games, not all children may be performing exactly the same task. The spirit of cooperation affords an opportunity for discussion and permits the players to negotiate in order to reach an agreement between the players. This is arrived at either verbally or through trial and error as different tasks are exercised in order to achieve the common goal. This trial and error is an essential component in the learning process. It is the educator's role to provide varied and numerous opportunities for children to practise and explore means of achieving mutual goals through game situation. In the parachute game of Cat and Mouse, described in the next chapter, all those who are around the periphery work together to hide the mouse. Some children may need to lift their arms up while others bring their arms down. This must be decided individually in order to solve the common goal of hiding the mouse from the cat.

The Benefits of Cooperative Games

In a noncompetitive environment socioaffective and interpersonal skills are developed through the task of working together, learning from each other, and learning about each other. We believe that cooperative games provide an important opportunity for children to learn to develop these interpersonal skills. Problem solving as part of this development will have a positive impact on interpersonal intelligence (Gardner, 1983). These games give children an opportunity to solve problems and build on existing knowledge towards the discovery of solutions. These games foster an environment where children can learn through mutual goals. Studies from as early as 1951 have drawn the conclusion that games can enhance the development of cooperative skills(Glakas, 1991). Cooperative movement games give children an opportunity to learn:

1. from each other
2. to adapt to other children's way of doing things
3. to work together and deal with compromise
4. through movement experiences without the threat of being eliminated.

Cooperative games will provide an environment where, although movement skills are being taught, there is a far greater and more important learning occurring through the process of positive individual and social growth. These games may "provide countless opportunities to encounter and exhibit society's desirable (as well as undesirable) behaviours. Desirable behaviours include sharing, honesty, concern for others, respect for others' rights and feelings, and self-discipline"(Glakas, 1991, p.28). All cooperative games strive to avoid the hurt that comes from being left out or eliminated during game play. Those children that are eliminated first are often the ones that need the most practice and will benefit from hands-on experience.

It is through moving cooperatively that children are given a sense of responsibility for the well being of others. In an increasingly competitive society, cooperation is not only important, but essential for social success. In working together children learn the valuable skill of compromise. Cooperative games strive to promote collaboration between those individuals involved in the game(Grineski, 1989). This does not dilute individual potential to achieve, it helps children learn to reach their own potential by helping others.

Kotloff (1993) points to studies in the early 1970s on group dynamics and the importance of "developing an effective, cohesive group out of a collection of individuals"(p.18). The ability to teach this through cooperative and group games should not be underestimated. Cooperative games reduce waiting time for all children as there is whole group participation. Cooperative games enhance positive self esteem by giving children many opportunities to succeed.

Socialization is a process that develops through social interaction. Cooperative movement games provide opportunity for positive social interaction within the context of movement games. It is through these opportunities that children learn about expectations, creating and following rules, and getting along with their peers. All this plays an important part in the process of socialization as it is only through positive experiences that children can gain a better perception of themselves and develop a better self-concept.

Supportive and noncompetitive movement games will foster an atmosphere for positive growth and development. Within cooperative games still resides an opportunity for individuals to express their ideas and their ways of problem solving. It is also valuable to give children an opportunity to create variations of the games that are played as a means of developing cognitive and creative skills. "By reconstructing games, children can learn to compete against their own limits or to work together toward a common goal rather then competing against each other for the purpose of winning at any cost" (Glakas, 1991, p.29). Cooperative games reduce the pressures of competition and encourage prosocial behaviour. There are no winners or losers, all players are equal. Success is assured through group effort. By placing importance on group effort and the successes of working together through motor activities, we teach children about themselves and we teach them to appreciate others and their ways of carrying out motor tasks.

Success in cooperative games is often dependent on the educator's role. You should act as a guide or facilitator and not as someone in "charge." It is often quite a challenge to take a back seat and still be the driver.

The learning opportunities at the end of the chapter are meant to provide a sample of the many useful and beneficial cooperative games. We have tried to limit the selection of opportunities to those that require a minimum of equipment, can be played both indoors and outdoors, and will ensure fun for all. Review your observations prior to selecting games and opportunities for the children. This will assist you in determining the present level of skill competence within your group. Remember, try and select activities that are challenging, but within reach of successful completion. Selecting activities that include motor skills that are too difficult will only lead to frustration and as such will undo the positive benefits of cooperative games. We have suggested some age delineations, but these are meant only as guidelines which are based on personal experience. The ages may not correspond exactly to the group you are working with. Take into consideration each individual within your group and the way in which they interact with each other. This forms an important part of planning.

COMPETITIVE GAMES

This section of the chapter will focus on those group games which can be competitive in nature. Competitive nonelimination games must have the following criteria.

1. An individual or group of players has an opposing goal to that of another individual or group of players.
2. Within each group or team there is a common goal.
3. All players are actively involved in the game at all times.

There is an entire category of nonelimination competitive games that has tremendous cognitive and affective value. Competitive games include both partner games, such as tennis or squash, and team sports, such as volleyball and waterpolo. These are games with rules. We have chosen to limit our discussion to nonelimination competitive games as they require full participation. In games where players are eliminated as in dodgeball, valuable time is wasted sitting on the sidelines watching. Williams (1992) relegates dodgeball, a game whose main purpose is to injure someone and has more than half the children watching rather than playing, to the Physical Education Hall of Shame (PEHOS). As we mentioned earlier in this chapter, being on the sidelines does not provide opportunity for continued practice of either the motor skills or the social skills that can be developed through active participation in group games. Sitting on the sidelines only promotes boredom.

Relay races in the traditional format do not build cooperative skills or involve total participation. Each child performs alone and is being scrutinized by teammates (Schwager, 1992). In a relay race situation there is little room for true cooperative efforts and for teammates to help one another in play. You may say: *...but my children love relay races....* Look carefully, it is more than likely that it is the child who is the more skilled athlete that truly likes relay races (Schwager, 1992).

In the nonelimination cooperative games the group does not necessarily work towards a common goal or end achievement. There can be an individual winner as in a racquet sport, or a team winner in a sport such as soccer. The important point here is that the emphasis is NOT placed on the "winning," it is placed on the play itself.

As with cooperative games, different players may be assigned a variety of roles. For competitive team games to work effectively, there must be a team effort. It is important to provide individuals with experiences that will promote a sense of good sportsmanship. You need to carefully examine the end product of a game in order to evaluate the process of learning that may occur during play. In team games and sports children need to draw on cooperative skills to achieve their team's goal.

Nonelimination competitive games also have rules that can be adhered to or modified. The impetus for change should come from the children's initiative. We believe that the challenge lies not in "winning", but in solving problems. Kamii and Devries (1984) contend that in group games children should have something both interesting and challenging to figure out. This of course infers problem solving, which results in a positive impact on children's cognitive development. Children do not set out to solve problems, nor do they have "motor goals." They set out to have fun. You should provide the ideas and environment to promote this. You can guide children to initiate their own play. For in " a play based approach to motor skills acquisition" (Trawick-Smith, p. 247), you help children construct ideas about the world around them, about each other, and promote body-kinaesthetic intelligence. These are powerful tools for enhancing social development.

CHAPTER HIGHLIGHTS

During the last few years, there has been an increased awareness and support for the concept of hands-on learning, whole group participation, and cooperation. Many schools today focus on cooperative learning. In the area of motor development both cooperative and group games have changed the way many educators design and implement the activities in their classroom. We encourage you to redesign the games you are presently using. Only your imagination will limit your efforts.

Keep in mind a few basic principles. Firstly, there should be provision for all to participate. There should be some form of common goal, either within a team, or from the group as a whole. Children should feel comfortable enough to take risks in their decision making process without any sense of reprisal. As much as is developmentally appropriate for the age group you are working with, children should be permitted to redesign rules and restructure their games. Children need to know that whatever decision they make, you will look favourably at it. Finally, do not be afraid to give up control.

LEARNING OPPORTUNITIES

1. ‖ <u>Cooperative Hot Potato</u>

Ages: three years and up

Ratio: three to four years, one to eight
five years and up, one to ten

Procedure:

Children are seated in a circle on the floor. Each child is given an object (small ball, beanbag etc.). Begin the music. Each child passes the object to the child on his right. When the music stops a child or children holding more then one object will take one of their objects out of the game. The game continues until there are no objects left.

Variation # 1

Use different coloured beanbags and decide before the music begins which colour beanbag will be eliminated. This should be done before each turn.

Variation # 2

Use only one object. When the music stops the child holding the object tosses it to another child sitting across from him. The game begins again.

focus: cooperation, manipulation, directional awareness

2. ‖   <u>Musical Hoops</u>

Ages: three years and up

Ratio: three to four years, one to eight
five years and up, one to ten

Procedure:

A variety of hoops are spread out on the floor. Begin with one per child or one for every two children. Begin the music. The children move to the music any way they please. When the music stops, the children are asked to step inside a hoop or touch the edge of the hoop with their foot. It is important to explain to the children that more than one child can stand in a hoop. Before starting the music again remove one hoop. The game continues until all but one hoop is left. As the number of hoops decreases, the children are encouraged to find creative ways of all touching a part of the hoop.

Variation # 1 <u>Musical Chairs</u>

Chairs are used rather then hoops and the children share the chairs.   The children don't necessarily need to be sitting on the chair, they can be touching the chair or sitting on someone's lap, etc.

focus: cooperation, locomotor skills, directional awareness, auditory awareness

3. ‖   <u>Red Light Green Light</u>

Ages: three years and up

Ratio: three to four years, one to eight
five years and up, one to ten

Procedure:

The children are asked to move freely around the room when they hear "Green Light". When they hear "Red Light" they have to freeze on the spot. The first caller should be the educator and then when they seem familiar with the game the children can have a turn calling out "Red Light" and " Green Light".

Variation # 1

Instead of calling out "Red Light" or "Green Light" a musical instrument can be used to stop and start the game.

Variation # 2

Two children share one hoop. They walk around the room inside the same hoop, stopping on red light and going on green light.

focus: nonelimination, locomotor skills, directional awareness

4. ‖ <u>Spud</u>

> **Age**: three and a half to five years
>
> **Ratio:** one to ten
>
> **Procedure:**
>
> In this game there are two equal lines of children facing each other. Lines should be about 3 feet (1 meter) apart. The game begins when the first child rolls (or kicks) the ball to the child across from him. This child then rolls the ball to the child diagonally across from him(see the diagram below). Tthe ball continues to be rolled until it reaches the last child. The last child then puts the ball in the basket that is situated at the end of the two lines. The child at the end of the line comes to the front of the line and everyone moves down one position. The game continues until everyone has had a chance to put the ball into the basket. For older children this game can be played against time, with everyone working to better the group time.

X   X   X   X   X

basket

X   X   X   X   X

Variation # 1

Once the children understand the concept of the game introduce more and more balls so that there is a continuous flow of kicking. (This eliminates the problem of any child waiting too long for their turn.)

focus: cooperation, locomotor skills, directional awareness

5. ‖   Bubble Tag

Ages: four years and up

Ratio: one to ten

Procedure:

One person is "it." A good idea is to have the educator start off as "it" until everyone understands the game. To start, the person who is "it" runs after the other children and tries to stick himself to another child. The two children then remain stuck together and run after the remaining children until a third child is stuck. This continues until all the children are stuck to each other in one large blob. The blob tries to move around the room until the children decide they have had enough.

Variation #1

Rather then sticking to each other children hold hands when they are touched by "it." The game continues until everyone is holding hands.

Variation #2

This is the same as variation #2 but in the water. We call it the "Octopus."

focus: cooperation, locomotor skills, directional awareness, spatial awareness

6. ‖   Kick That Ball

Ages: four years and up

Ratio: one to ten

Procedure:

Children stand in a circle either holding hands or with arms around each other. They begin to kick a ball back and forth across the circle to one another. The ball must stay within the perimeter of the circle.

Variation #1

Same formation as above. The ball is placed in the centre of the circle and must stay within the circle. The group tries to move the ball from one end of the room or outdoor playing area to the other.

note: This game is lots of fun with a large beach ball.

focus: cooperation, manipulation, directional awareness, spatial awareness

7. ‖ <u>Squirrel</u>

    Ages: four years and up

    Ratio: one to ten

    Procedure:

Children stand or sit in a circle. There are two boxes. One is placed at the beginning of the circle and one at the end of the circle. (The boxes are actually side by side.) One box is full of items and one box is empty. The game begins when the first child takes an item out of the box and passes the item to the child on his right. This procedure continues until there are no items left in the box. The more varied the size, shape and weight of the objects, the more fun the game is. When the last child gets the item it is placed in the empty box. The game continues until the full box is empty and the empty box is full.

focus: cooperation, fine motor manipulation, directional awareness

8. ‖ <u>Red Rover</u>

    Ages: four years and up

    Ratio: one to ten

    Procedure:

Children are all standing in a line holding hands. The child at one end of the line begins the game by starting to weave through the line of children while still holding hands with the other children.
While going through, the children chant:
      Red Rover, Red Rover weave on over
      Red Rover, Red Rover weave on through
The chain of children is continuous, with no beginning and no end. The challenge of the game is to work together so that the chain of hands is not broken. When the chain is broken the game begins again.

focus: cooperation, directional awareness, spatial awareness, locomotor skills

9. ‖ <u>Modified Frozen Tag</u>

Ages: four and a half years and up

Ratio: one to ten

Procedure:

Depending on the size of the group one or more children are designated as "it." The "it" chases the other children and tries to touch them. If a child is tagged, they have to FREEZE. Holding still is an important motor skill requiring the use of static balance. The other children can unfreeze them by touching them. The educator should rotate the "it" child so that everyone can have a turn.

Variation # 1

The game is played the same way except that to unfreeze a frozen child the other child must crawl under their legs, rather then just touching him.

Variation # 2

Give the children scarves to attach loosly tuck into a pair of pants, belt or skirt. The child who is "it" must grab the scarf from behind the child wearing it and put it on the ground. The child now without the scarf is frozen. Any child who is still free can unfreeze other children by picking up his scarf and returning it to him.

focus: cooperation, balance, locomotor skills, spatial awareness

10. ‖ <u>Mirroring</u>

Ages: four to eight years

Ratio: one to ten

Procedure:

Children are divided into pairs with one child facing the other. The educator works with a child if there is an odd number in the class. The educator should change the child they are working with periodically so that all can have an opportunity to work with their peers. One child initiates movement(s) while the other is the mirror image.

Variation # 1

Children are given suggestions of feelings or events to express through open-ended directions. Examples: How do you move first thing in the morning? How do you move when you are playing outside? How do you move when you are happy, sad, tired, wide awake, etc. These instructions should be given one at a time.

Encourage children to create their own movements and communicate non-verbally.

focus: partner activity, cooperation, balance, body awareness

11. ‖ <u>Sally Says</u>

    Ages: four years and up

    Ratio: one to ten

    Procedure:

Divide the class into two groups. A caller instructs everyone to move a part of the body, for example, "shake your fanny." If someone misses a cue he simply changes teams. Play continues until one team is much larger than the other.

focus: nonelimination, auditory awareness, body awareness

12. ‖ <u>Crows and Cranes</u>

    Ages: four years and up

    Ratio: one to ten

    Procedure:

Divide the children into two groups facing each other on either side of the room. One group is called "Crows" and the other group is called "Cranes." The game begins when the educator calls out either "Crows" or "Cranes." If the educator calls out "Cranes" the "Cranes" get to run around the room. When the educator calls "Crows" the "Crows" get to run around the room. The children stop in their place when the educator calls any other name beginning with the first three letters of the word "crane" such as, "Cra..." If a crow moves when a crane is called out, he change teams. If a crane moves when crow is called out, he changes teams.

focus: nonelimination, auditory awareness, locomotor skills

13. ‖ <u>Partner Pull-Up</u>

Ages: four years and up

Ratio: partner activity

Procedure:

Two children about the same size and weight are sitting on the floor facing each other, knees bent and toes touching. When they are ready to begin, they hold each other's hands. They try to stand up at the same time without letting go of each other's hands.

Variation # 1

Once this task is mastered, the children can be encouraged to follow the same instructions while back to back and arms interlocked (see Learning Opportunity # 18)

focus: cooperation, balance, muscular strength

14. ‖ <u>Circle Untangle</u>

Age: eight years and up

Ratio: one to ten

Procedure:

Stand in a circle. Instruct each person to hold hands with any two people in the circle except those immediately next to him. The object of the game is to untangle everyone without letting go of each other's hands. In the end a perfect circle is formed with everyone holding hands. Oh, yes, you cannot let go of each others hands while trying to become untangled.

focus: cooperation, directional awareness

15. ‖ Switch

Age: eight and up

Ratio: twelve to one

Procedure:

The players form rows of four or five children, depending on the number in your group. The children all hold hands except one child who is the cat and one child who is the mouse. The rows of children try to prevent the mouse from being caught. The children can only run up and down the lines that are created by the children holding hands. They cannot run under anyone's arms or break the lines. When any child sees the cat getting too close to the mouse, they yell "switch" and everyone in the group must turn around 90 degrees to face the other way and rejoin hands. This changes the rows to face the other direction so that the cat gets trapped in a different row than the mouse is in. Any child can yell "switch" who is in a position to decide what is best for the mouse.

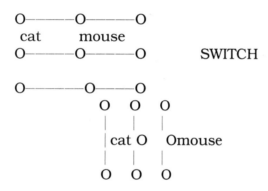

focus: cooperation, locomotor skills, directional awareness

REFERENCES

Gardner, Howard (1983) *Frames of Mind.* New York: Basic Books.

Glakas, Barbara A. (1991) "Teaching Cooperative Skills Through Games," *Journal of Physical Education and Recreation.* June 28-30.

Grineski, Steven (1989) "Children, Games and Prosocial Behaviour-Insight and Connections", *Journal of Physical Education Recreation and Dance,* Oct. 1989.

Kamii, Constance & Devries, Rheta (1984) *Group Games in Early Education, Implications of Piaget's Theory.* Washington: NAEYC.

Kotloff, Lauren J. (1993) Fostering Cooperative Group Spirit and Individuality: Examples From a Japanese Preschool," *Young Children*, March, pp.17-23, NAEYC.

Lay-Dopyera, Margaret & Dopyera, John (1990) *Becoming a Teacher of Young Children*, (4th ed) New York: McGraw Hill.

Moore, Dorothy L. (1986) "The Winning Alternative, Solving the Dilemma of the Win/Lose Syndrome," *Childhood Education*, January/February.

Nicholos, Beverly (1990) *Moving and Learning*. St. Louis, Times Mirror/Mosby College Publishing.

Pangrazi, Robert P. & Dauer, Victor P. (1981) *Movement in Early Childhood and Primary Education*. Minneapolis, Minesota: Burgess Publishing Company.

Schwager, Susan (1992) "Relay Races - Are They Appropriate for Elementary Physical Education?" *Journal of Physical Education, Recreation, and Dance.*Reston: Virginia: American Alliance for Health, Physical Education, Recreation and Dance. August, vol.63:6.

Trawick-Smith (1994) *Interactions in the Classroom, Facilitating Play in the Early Years*. Don Mills, Ontario: Maxwell MacMillan

Williams, Neil F. (1992) "The Physical Education Hall of Shame" *Journal of Physical Education, Recreation, and Dance*. Reston, Virginia: American Alliance for Health, Physical Education, Recreation and Dance. August, vol.63:6.

Chapter 10
THE PARACHUTE

In this chapter you will learn about:

- The parachute
- Perceptual motor development
- Physical fitness
- Gross/fine motor development
- Schoolage
- Nonelimination/cooperative skills
- Guidance
- Learning opportunities

PARACHUTE PLAY

The parachute gives new meaning to some of the old familiar action songs.

Robert Pangrazi and Victor Dauer

THE PARACHUTE

The parachute is a wonderful and extremely versatile piece of equipment. We ask you to reflect for a moment: *What type of image do you have when you hear the word parachute? Do you think of people with parachutes on their backs or sky divers ready to jump out of a plane?*

The parachute that we will discuss is the same piece of equipment that is used by sky divers. Its use, described in this chapter, is very different. It is both ingenious and multipurpose. It can be used indoors and outdoors to develop perceptual motor domains, increase physical fitness, enhance gross/fine motor development, and provide cooperative nonelimination experiences that will foster interpersonal skills. Most importantly, the parachute is great fun and can easily be adapted for use with all ages.

Parachutes used in educational settings are made of the same nylon fabric as the skydiver's parachutes and are constructed in much the same way. They are round and vary in diameter from six to twenty-four feet (1.8 to 7.3 meters). We suggest a nine foot parachute for indoor use and an eighteen to twenty-four-foot (5.4 to 7.3 meters) parachute for outdoor use. Parachutes can be purchased in combinations of two colours or many bright colours.

All parachute designs are quite similar with only a few variations. Some are designed with handles along the perimeter for children to hold on to, while others require that the individual hold on to the outer edge of the fabric. Those with handles on the perimeter tend to limit the number of children that can participate as each child will want to grasp a handle. Furthermore, the handles do not lend themselves to the same variety of grips.

Another variation is that some have a hole in the centre. This hole can be used to your advantage in creating activities. Roll balls on top of the parachute and try to keep them away from the hole or, conversely, try to get a ball through the hole. Those with the holes trap the air differently than do the others. This means that when you lift up the parachute and bring it down the bubble effect will be slightly different. We do not have a preference of one type over the other but we suggest that each has its advantages. In some centres there are two parachutes, one of each design.

PERCEPTUAL MOTOR DEVELOPMENT

The parachute is a piece of equipment that lends itself to tactile experiences. The texture is unique and participants learn how this lightweight piece of fabric responds to their movements. The parachute traps air in interesting ways. Exploring the feel and texture of the fabric lends itself to good use of descriptive vocabulary. Many adjectives can be used to describe the parachute. Some words are: smooth, soft, slippery, or thin.

The parachute does not respond the same way indoors as it will outdoors. In northern climates, a cold crisp day will affect the way in which the fabric responds to the group effort. The cold causes the fabric to become more rigid and creates different sounds as it is being used. It crackles and snaps as it is shaken up and down.

Introductory parachute activities should include a discussion of how the material feels, allowing children time to touch, manipulate, and respond and then volunteer their opinions. You may want to consider comparison with other fabrics such as scarves, which can then be used as an introductory opportunity.

This piece of equipment takes up a great deal of space and occupies space very differently from other equipment. Some learning opportunities, such as Mushroom, actually create a unique space for the child to enter. In Mushroom, an intimate, closed environment is constructed. The following anecdote describes an interesting discussion that occurred while in the mushroom. The children in this sample were four years old.

♦ ♦ ♦

We lifted the parachute up and brought it down behind our backs and over our heads. Everyone sat on the floor inside the parachute. Joelle shouted out, "Where did the space go?" David answered confidently, "It's out there, on top of us!"

♦ ♦

Photo 10.1. Getting into the mushroom.

Children love to help create the mushroom. Some children enjoy holding on to and manouevering the parachute. Others like to run around inside the newly formed space. Once inside the mushroom, all the children discover the interesting effects formed as a result of their own manipulations of the apparatus. This exciting parameter adds greatly to the experience. You can engage in discussions later in the day that include conversations about why the parachute holds its shape in the air for a time before floating down, or about how it feels to be inside. The Mushroom is one of the many activities suitable for both same age and mixed age grouping.

In the photo on the next page, you will notice that the light easily filters through the parachute. Children usually feel quite safe and secure inside the parachute bubble.

Photo 10.2. Children enjoying the newly created space.

Through games such as Magic Cloud, which create spaces for the child to lie, sit or run under, spatial and temporal awareness are developed. Indoors, the air traps the parachute and it stays on the ceiling for a time. You are never quite sure where it will land, yielding interesting discussion and often excitement. Outdoors, the parachute does not necessarily go straight up because it is influenced by the wind and weather. The time it takes to come down will vary depending on how much force is used to send it up in the air. The amount of force used to lift the parachute and the size of the parachute directly affect how high it will go.

The parachute changes shape as it is lifted in the air, creating an interesting visual field. In outdoor play, the wind helps the parachute change form. It can move fast or slow. It can be made to move with a jerky or sudden action when pulled taut and shaken. Watch the parachute glide down with sustained action! During free play, you can put out scarves and other lightweight fabrics for the children to explore. The children can toss the fabrics in the air and watch how they are effected by the air. Excellent explorations and discussions arise through comparison of the various fabrics with the parachute.

Directional awareness is developed as the children move their arms up and down, as they walk around, to the left and to the right. Some Learning Opportunities require all the participants to walk in one direction at a time, such as Ring Around the Rosie or the Wheels on the Bus. In other Learning Opportunities, such as Changing Places, directional cue words such as run across or go to the other side are used.

PHYSICAL FITNESS

Most parachute activities will have a positive impact on physical fitness. During many of the parachute activities there are repetitive movements that use the large muscles of the body. These movements increase the heart rate and stimulate the cardiovascular system as well as increase muscular strength and endurance.

For example, in the activity Lift Off, the children are running with the parachute to keep it up in the air and, of course, the faster you run the higher it goes. Running and supporting the parachute in the air both contribute to the positive development of physical fitness. Best of all, Lift Off is a blast!

Photo 10.3. Children enjoy Lift Off.

In many of the activities you are required to continuously lift the parachute up and bring it back down again. To accomplish this the individuals in the group must lift their arms up and down from the shoulder area. These movements result in strengthening the both the shoulder region and the upper body. As mentioned in Chapter 3, this is an area which is often neglected.

In the Learning Opportunity Cat and Mouse, all the children are involved in some form of active participation. The continuous actions of arms of those at the perimeter, and the racing across or under the parachute, all contribute to positive development of physical fitness. Since the heart rate is kept elevated throughout, there is also a focus on cardiovascular endurance.

Muscular endurance increases gradually with the parachute. As you use the parachute more often you will notice that the children will be able to sustain movements for a longer period of time. This in turn will lead to longer and more fruitfull experiences with the apparatus.

GROSS/FINE MOTOR DEVELOPMENT

Holding the parachute provides an opportunity to develop fine motor skills. The different types of grasps exercise and strengthen the muscles in the hands and fingers. The various grasps include an overhand or underhand palmar grasp and a mixed grasp. In either situation, the entire hand closes around the parachute. In this way, the muscles of the fingers and hands are strengthened and there is an increase in fine motor control. Increased strength in the muscles of the hand and fingers will assist in refining fine motor development in other areas of day-to-day life.

Many of the opportunities increase gross motor development while focusing on a variety of locomotor and non locomotor movements. The accent and the focus of the games vary. Some games involve emphasis of the large muscles of the upper body, while other activities involve whole body actions. Other games require a combination of whole body actions while travelling from one spot to another. Individuals can practise locomotor skills of crawling, walking, running, and jumping to name a few.

There are many simple activities that require the children to walk around the parachute. Specific Learning Opportunities such as Alligator, focuses on locomotor skills. In this Opportunity, children crawl under the parachute in a restricted space. Gross motor actions are called into play as each child slinks across under the parachute.

The children who are keeping the parachute level and taut must use their hands and fingers to hold on firmly.

Photo 10.4. Children actively manipulate the parachute.

In the Learning Opportunity Climbing the Mountain, children develop their upper bodies as they are encouraged to lift the parachute up and then push the trapped air down with their arms, shaping the parachute into a mountain. This game works best with the medium or large parachute. Then the children are asked to climb the mountain and to lift their legs very high stretching to their maximum, as they move in towards the centre of the parachute trying to climb to the other side. Besides fostering gross motor development, the parachute has a terrific potential for cognitive growth. We played this game with a group of four-year-old children, using an eighteen foot (5.5 meters) parachute and had the following experience:

♦ ♦ ♦

The children were gathered around the parachute. We lifted the parachute up, then brought it down quickly to the ground, placing our knees on the edge. A great bubble was created. All the children were asked to push the parachute down, first with their arms. They were then asked to move in towards the centre of the parachute. Dan exclaimed gleefully, "Look, the air moved!"

♦ ♦

Needless to say, a wonderful discussion ensued. *Where did the air go? What do you think happened?* These are teachable moments. Use children's natural curiosity and excitement to stimulate thinking. Every question a child has is valuable. Helping children discover is the only way to keep them interested and curious. Nonlocomotor movements are seen in many of the games as the children bend at the waist or at the knees in order to lift the parachute up. Bending, twisting, and stretching are also required in most of the parachute activities.

SCHOOLAGE

Schoolage children continue to enjoy the parachute and their increased attention span makes it possible to interact with it longer then preschool children. Your role becomes very different with this age group of children. Generally speaking, school age children will have already had some previous experience. They are therefore familiar with the parachute and maybe using it in their regular gym class. It is extremely important that they be allowed to select activities for themselves. When children have an activity that they would like to share, it is important that they be allowed to explain it to the group, describing the movements and what everyone needs to do. As the educator, your role becomes one of facilitator and guide. Offer support, assistance, and become familiar with the activities your group enjoys. You can provide an extra challenge by encouraging them to redesign or combine existing games in order to make new ones. At this age you can move beyond the games and begin to choreograph a variety of movements to popular music. Using a piece of music that the group as a whole enjoys, invite the children to interpret the music and design movements that correspond to the rhythm and beat. For example, a strong rhythmic beat may suggest lifting the parachute up while some children run from one side to the other. Another rhythm might make you feel like shaking the parachute very quickly. As the children show an interest in this type of activity you can encourage them to count the beats of the music and they can determine how many beats to hold or repeat a movement, resulting in a choreographed effect...a performance that is arrived at through a cooperative group effort.

NONELIMINATION/COOPERATIVE SKILLS

An important feature of the parachute is that it provides for nonelimination type activities and it enhances cooperation and interpersonal skills. Parachute play can meet the requirements of cooperative games as described in the previous chapter. The group manipulates a large piece of equipment and works together to achieve a mutually agreed upon goal. As with all cooperative games, there is no elimination process and everyone participates. Children and adults all work together towards a common goal. They interact with one another through language and verbal exchange in order to find ways to manipulate the parachute and achieve their common goal. Parachute play is only successful when individuals function as a team. Whether performing the same or different tasks, there is a synchrony of movement and an understanding of direction that takes place. Children quickly understand how the parachute responds to group effort.

If the group lifts their arms up together, the parachute goes up high, responding to everyone's movements. To tilt the parachute, some players need to lift it up while others bring it down. There are no winners or losers and an atmosphere for success is created. This in turn builds positive self-esteem and self-image. Successful team efforts yield a sense of accomplishment.

Some parachute games can be competitive in nature. We recommend turning the focus around to meet cooperative goals of parachute play. For example, in the game of Cat and Mouse, the emphasis is not on the cat catching the mouse. Rather, as explained earlier it is on the group as a whole working towards the common goal of hiding the mouse. The objective is to hide the mouse for as long as possible by creating great big air pockets. When working with school age children you may discover competitive parachute games. Ensure that they meet the criteria of nonelimination games for maximum effectiveness. This will help reach goals of positive self-esteem and whole group participation.

GUIDANCE

We often find that educators have a misconception surrounding the issues of guidance and the parachute. Many educators shy away from using the parachute for fear they will be unable to "control" the group. Two points come to mind. Firstly, consider *what does control mean?* Often we are afraid of activities that are too loud, fearing we have lost "control" of a group. Or we may be upset if all the children do not wish to participate. Consider the noise level and excitement as part of the fun. Try to have alternatives for those who do not wish to participate or just give them time they may need to warm up and become comfortable about joining in. Another issue related to control is that too often we have a preconceived idea of what activities and in what progression they should be presented. We suggest a flexible approach where you adapt to the will of the group.

Secondly, there are many lead up activities that can be carried out that gradually introduce the skills needed for success with the parachute. Moving individually to music with scarf in hand will simulate the motions needed in playing with the parachute. Encourage children to lift the scarf first with one hand then the other. Ask them to try holding a different end of the scarf with each hand and lifting their arms up and down or move them from side to side. As this is done on an individual basis, the added challenge of working cooperatively is not yet introduced. From here, you might want to introduce the six-foot (1.8 meter) parachute.

We also suggest that just before the parachute is brought out for the children to use the educator should consider letting the children know about this special piece of equipment. Discuss its size, how it requires that everyone work together and help each other, and talk about how much fun it is. With this small size the children are really close together and it is easy to make eye contact with each child as you guide the group. After demonstrating the use of the parachute, we like to leave it within easy access for the children. Let them decide on their own if they wish to pursue it. We find children learn a great deal by playing independently with their peers.

Try and incorporate songs that are familiar to the children with the parachute. Such common songs include "Ring Around the Rosie, The Wheels on The Bus, and The Grand Old Duke of York." This approach models Piaget's theory that "development is solidly rooted in what already exists and displays a continuity with the past"(Baldwin, p.139).

Most of all, relax and have fun with it yourself. Modelling a positive attitude will provide good incentive for the children to be positive as well. Participate actively in all the activities and we guarantee you success.

CHAPTER HIGHLIGHTS

The parachute is a unique and fascinating piece of equipment that can provide hours of endless fun and enjoyment for all ages. Younger children especially enjoy sitting in the middle while the other children and adults turn them around and sing a song as in Tug Boat. Older children usually prefer a more vigorous type of activity such as running underneath playing games like Lift Off and Cat and Mouse. The parachute can be used indoors or outdoors, with a small group or a large one. It can be used sitting down or as a warmup or cooldown activity.

The parachute is an extremely valuable piece of equipment in that it can be contribute positively to perceptual motor development, enhance all areas of fundamental skill development, increase physical fitness, and improve balance. Perhaps its most unique characteristic is its use as an effective tool towards the development of cooperative learning skills and its emphasis on inclusion rather than exclusion. This is truly and all around piece of equipment

See Appendix C for information on purchasing parachutes and a video.

LEARNING OPPORTUNITIES

INTRODUCTORY OPPORTUNITIES

1. ‖   Scarves

     Age: two and a half years and up

     Ratio: two and a half to four, one to eight
                   four years and up, one to ten

Procedure:

Bring out colourful scarves, ribbons, or streamers. Ensure that there is at least one per child. Have everyone lift the scarves up and down. Explore the patterns that the scarf can make in the air. The up and down arm motions resemble some of the movements needed when working with the parachute. Introduce some music and have the children move their scarf rhythmically to the beat of the music.

focus: nonlocomotor, locomotor, manipulation, auditory perception

2. ‖ <u>Exploration</u>

    Age: two to five years

    Ratio: two to three years, one to six
                      four to five years, one to eight

Procedure:

Place the parachute in a mound on the floor and ask questions: What does the parachute feel like? Does this fabric feel like any other? Suggest that the children all pull the parachute open. State: Let's see how big it is? What shape is the parachute? Let us all pull the parachute tightly towards us. Shake your hands and watch what happens to the parachute. How can you make low waves, high waves? Lift your arms way above your head. What happens to the parachute. What shape does it make? Let's call this shape a great big cloud. What happens when there are many big clouds? (wait for a response) Rain! Begin this rhythmic chant or any other you know that you feel will work:

The rain is falling down SPLAT!
    (at this cue bring the parachute down)
The sun is coming up Yeah!
    (at this cue bring the parachute up)

Repeat 3 or 4 times.

Shake like this and shake like that
    (using both arms shake the parachute vigorously)
...now we stop this way.
    (on this cue, all sit down)

focus: nonelimination, cooperation, manipulation, auditory perception, tactile awareness

3. ‖ <u>Connected</u>

    Age: all

    Ratio: will vary depending on the age of the children

    Procedure:

You will need fifteen to twenty feet (four and a half to six meters) of a four-inch (10 centimeter) wide elastic band. Tie the two ends together to make a circle. Everyone takes hold of a part of the elastic so that you are all standing around a circle. First, stretch the band out and walk in a circle singing your favourite song. Now walk the other way. Lift the elastic over-head. Hold your arms up high and stretch your two hands away from your ears. The resistance of the elastic gives the arms a good stretch and strengthens the shoulder and arms. Now everyone comes into the centre of the circle and moves back again, stretching the elastic out. Lift elastic behind your head and put it behind your back. Make up your own ideas with the elastic band.(Source: Helen Panagiotopolous)

focus: nonelimination, locomotor skills, manipulation

Learning opportunities for further growth and development

4. ‖ Tug Boat

> **Age:**　　　　eighteen months to four years
>
> **Ratio:**　　　eighteen months to two years, one to one
> 　　　　　　　　two to three 3 years, two to eight
> 　　　　　　　　four years, two to ten

Procedure:

One or two children are placed in the middle of the parachute. The other children stand around the parachute, holding it with a palmar grasp. Children are asked to walk around in the same direction while singing the following song.
Song: *TUG BOAT, TUG BOAT, GO SO SLOW.*
　　　TUG BOAT, TUG BOAT, GO SO FAST.
　　　TUG BOAT, TUG BOAT, OUT OF GAS...
At this point the children stop walking around, kneel or squat down, shake the parachute, and sing.
　　　FILL IT UP, FILL IT UP
　　　FILL IT UP FAST
　　　FILL IT UP WITH GAS.....
This causes the parachute to turn, giving those on it a ride. Continue until all the children have had a turn.

focus: manipulation, directional awareness, locomotor skills

5. ‖ Cooperative Balls

> **Age:**　　　　three to five years
>
> **Ratio:**　　　one to eight

Procedure:

Each child sits on the floor holding onto the parachute. They each choose a ball and place it in front of them on the floor. The children then start making little waves by shaking the parachute. The educator calls a child's name. That child throws her ball onto the parachute. This continues until all balls are circulating simultaneously. You can sing a verse to the tune of "The Wheels on the Bus" by Raffi: *The balls on the parachute go round and round, round and round, early in the morning.*

focus: manipulation, auditory perception, nonelimination, cooperation.

6. ‖ <u>Boat out at Sea</u>

 Age: three to five years

 Ratio: two to three years, one to six
       four to five years, one to eight

Procedure:

The children are seated around the parachute, holding onto the edge. They are instructed to shake the parachute lightly, then more vigorously, making smaller and larger waves. You all pretend that the parachute is the sea. A ball is placed in the sea and it represents the boat. Chant: *there is a boat out at sea.* The waves created by shaking the parachute will make the ball roll. A big wind comes and pushes the ball /boat from one side of the sea to the other. The boat can rock from side to side. To conclude, roll ball back to shore. Shore is the perimeter of the parachute. This facilitates retrieving the balls at the end of the experience.

focus: fine motor manipulation, nonlocomotor, auditory perception, non-elimination, cooperation.

7. ‖ <u>Changing Places</u>

 Ages: three and up

 Ratio: three to five years, two to ten
       six years and up, two to fourteen

Procedure:

Children stand and hold parachute with any grip. Introduce a song such as: The People on the Bus Go Up and Down. On <u>UP</u>, everyone lifts the parachute together then lets it float down slowly. This is repeated. Call out a colour that some children are wearing. Those wearing that colour change places with each other before the chute comes down over their heads. Let the children have a turn to be a caller. For variation tell children to find a new way of getting across under the parachute.

focus: locomotor skills, manipulation, auditory perception, nonelimination

8. ‖ Alligator Game

> **Ages:**   four years and up
>
> **Ratio:**   one to ten

Procedure:

The children are seated on the floor around the parachute. Legs stretched straight under the parachute. Hands are tightly holding the parachute up at their chin level, using an overhand palmar grasp.

The game begins with one child crawling around under the parachute. The child crawling finds a pair of legs under the parachute and touches them. Once a child has successfully touched another child's leg, she comes out from under the parachute and take that child's place and sits with her legs crossed. The new child (the child who just had his legs touched) goes under the parachute and repeats the same process. The game continues until all legs are crossed or everyone has had a turn.

focus: manipulation, locomotor skills, nonelimination, cooperation.

9. ‖ Popcorn

> **Ages:**   four years and up
>
> **Ratio:**   four to five years, one to eight
>   six years and up, one to twelve

Procedure:

In this game different balls can be used such as nerf balls or balloons, etc. Balls (representing the popcorn) are placed on the parachute. Children stand around the parachute and begin to shake it up and down so that the balls bounce. Two different sets of instructions can be used. The children can try to keep the popcorn on the parachute, or they can try to pop all the balls off the parachute. The second option works better outdoors.

focus: gross motor manipulation, nonelimination, cooperation

10. ‖ Climbing over the Mountain

Age: all

Ratio: will vary depending on the age of the children

Procedure:

Children stand around the parachute. They lift it up once or twice, quickly bringing it back down to the floor. The fast movement results in air being captured under the parachute and it creates a mountain-like appearance. Once the mountain appears one or two children are asked to climb over the mountain to the other side. The activity is repeated until everyone has had a turn.

focus: balance, locomotor skills, manipulation, nonelimination

11. ‖ Cat and Mouse

Ages: four years and up

Ratio: four to six years years, one to eight
seven years and up, one to twelve

Procedure:

One child "the cat" goes under the chute and "the mouse" goes on top. The mouse has to try and get away from the cat. The other children shake the parachute so that air pockets are created and the mouse is concealed under them. The game ends when the cat catches the mouse. Then another child is designated as the cat and another as the mouse.

focus: gross motor manipulation, locomotor skills, nonelimination, cooperation.

12. ‖ <u>Magic Cloud</u>

> **All**: all
>
> **Ratio:** two/three adults to ten/fourteen

Procedure:

Younger children: The educator manipulates the parachute. Children lie on their backs on the floor under the parachute. The educators lift the parachute up high over their heads three times. On the third lift, the educators let go of the parachute so that it floats away in the air and then lands on or near the children who are lying on the floor.

Older children: Standing around the parachute they all lift it over their heads and count "1, 2, 3...cloud dust". Release the parachute. Try to catch it as it floats back down.

focus: nonlocomotor, manipulation, nonelimination

13. ‖ <u>Lift Off</u>

> **Age:** four years and up
>
> **Ratio:** eight to one

Procedure:

This opportunity is best played outside where there is plenty of space to run. The children stand on one side of a large parachute with their backs towards the apparatus. They hold onto the parachute behind them. When everyone is ready, the educator gives the signal for the children to run. They all go in the same direction with the parachute trailing behind them. As the children pick up speed, the wind will lift the parachute off the ground and into the air. Younger children can play this individually using a small parachute.

focus: physical fitness, running, cooperation, nonelimination

REFERENCES

Baldwin, A.L. (1980) *Theories of Child Development*, 2nd edition. New York: John Wiley & Sons Inc.

Gardner, Howard (1993) *Frames of Mind*, tenth edition. New York: Bantam Books.

Pangrazi, Robert P. & Dauer, Victor P. (1981) *Movement in Early Childhood and Primary Education.* Minneapolis, Minnesota: Burgess Publishing Company.

Chapter 11
CREATIVE MOVEMENT AND GUIDED FANTASY

In this chapter you will learn about:

- Perceptual components of creative movement
  - spatial awareness
  - directional awareness
  - body awareness
  - temporal awareness
- The goals and benefits of creative movement
- Beginning your creative movement session
- Relationships
- Guided Fantasy
- Imagery
- Learning Opportunities

CREATIVE MOVEMENT

Creative movement can help children to grow emotionally -- it helps children feel successful and appreciated because there is no right or wrong way to move.

Ginger Zukowski and Ardie Dickson

CREATIVE MOVEMENT

Laban (in Thorton, 1971) was the first to describe movement as emerging from an inner directed force known as *effort*. This effort was then subdivided into four categories of *space, weight, time, and flow*. All forms of creative movement and creative dance in Laban's description would fall into these categories. We have incorporated these classifications along with ours on perceptual motor development, and with Gardnerian ideology, in order to come up with a modern description of creative movement (Gardner, 1993; Thorton, 1971; Murdock, 1987).

Before beginning our description of creative movement, we felt it worthwhile to mention that creative movement provides the components for all forms of dance that are an important part of society and culture. Whether grounded in folklore, ballet, jazz, modern, or funk, each individual develops an understanding of dance based on his own experience(Lord and Bruneau, 1983). Creative movements provide the component parts for creative dance and many other dance forms. **Creative dance** is often the product of creative movement. It involves the combination of movements, steps, or patterns, which once choreographed, can be repeated. By this definition, our discussion of creative movement has relevance to any discussion of creative dance.

Laban's discussion of space includes the concepts of space and direction. For him, direction is a part of moving in space. We concur with his view, but have found it more effective to treat directional awareness as a separate topic. Many of the verbal cues used in directional awareness overlap with those that would be used in spatial awareness. Under spatial awareness we look at levels in space, such as high or low, and general and personal space, which include the entire space that is available for use and the immediate space that one individual can use. Under our heading of *directional awareness* we discuss spatial patterns. This includes the concept of pathways on the floor and the direction in which the body can move.

Under Laban's classification, weight refers to how the body absorbs weight and transfers it to different body parts. This area is discussed as a part of body awareness. In recalling our discussion on body awareness, this concept includes naming body parts, location of body parts, and understanding how they move in relation to one another.

Time, of course, will be discussed under the heading *temporal awareness*. This refers to speed of movement. Flow refers to the quality and energy given to a movement. Is the movement free flowing, jerky, or sustained? Flow will be included as a part of the discussion of temporal awareness.

We will add the subheading of *relationships* to our discussion of creative movement. Relationships refers to the interaction of self, partners, and groups; much the same categories that were discussed in nonelimination games.

The concepts itemized above all help develop body kinaesthetic intelligence, an understanding of how the body functions, how one learns through the body, and the attainment of a greater understanding of oneself and one's physical abilities through movement (Thorton, 1971; Gardner, 1993).

PERCEPTUAL COMPONENTS OF CREATIVE MOVEMENT

Spatial Awareness

Spatial knowledge includes an understanding of both general space and personal space. In creative movement, cues used to explore personal space and general space are different. Personal space of course refers to that space which is immediately around us, while general space refers to the space around us either in the room or outdoors. There is also outer space, which is very far away. Many words are used as cues to develop an understanding of spatial concepts. Those related to levels include:

high	....	*low*
middle	....	*bottom*

Those related to personal space include:

near	....	*far*
here	....	*there*

Words that help develop cognitive concepts of body shape in relation to space include:

curved	....	*straight*
wide	....	*thin*
fat	....	*flat*
small	....	*large*

Concepts, as usual, should be presented from simple to complex. For example, at three and four years old, ask children to curl up like a small ball; at five and six, ask them to pretend they are a ball that needs to be inflated. As the ball is inflated it grows larger and larger. Sometimes providing the image of a balloon is easier than using that of a ball. Concrete experiences help children acquire knowledge. For example, you can visually demonstrate by blowing up a balloon and discussing with the children what happens before asking them to physically interpret this experience. Older children can be given a balloon to blow up so they can experience how the air fills the space of rubber as it expands.

As a creative movement experience, ask the children to expand like a balloon. When they are ready, suggest that they turn into a ball, bouncing around the room. Ask questions that provoke reflection. *Does your ball bounce high or low?* By about seven, you can introduce the bouncing ball, utilizing cooperative effort between two children. Children are paired, one child is the ball, curled up small, while the other is playing with the ball and has to, through body language, instruct the ball how high to bounce.

Directional Awareness

Creating pathways on the floor, moving from side to side, moving forward and backward are ways to focus on directional awareness as it relates to ourselves. The use of vision to locate objects in space and to align oneself to an object in the space around us gives the feeling of direction as it relates to objects in space.

By practising moves of front and back or up and down, the child builds a directional orientation. By following objects such as scarves in dance, or balls on the ground, the child develops a sense of increased directional awareness and visual tracking. Encourage children to use the whole space that is provided whether in the gym or outdoors. As children get older, they have a tendency to move in a more restricted pattern and increasingly in the same direction. Let the children know where the empty space is in the room and tell them to fill it. Some cue words to help develop directional awareness include:

up	....	*down*
curved pattern	....	*straight pattern*
forward	....	*backward*
side to	....	*side*
change direction	....	*go back the way you came*

Body Awareness

The concept of body awareness was first introduced in Chapter 2. Creative movement provides one vehicle to develop those concepts related to body awareness. To assess if a child is developmentally ready for you to introduce creative movement and body awareness you might first determine if the child has a basic knowledge of where specific body parts are and how they move. It is not necessary that the child be able to name them at this point. The child should at least be able to identify some of the different parts of the body and move them in simple ways. As body awareness develops, combinations of movements can be used to stimulate integrated movements.

Funny directions can be used to add a lively dimension to movement exploration. Suggest leading an action with one body part, such as the arm or nose, and change the texture of the movement. This will serve to add some humour.

Interesting instructions can be given to help the children understand the ways in which their bodies can move. For example, lean to one side of the body, now lean to the other. This helps the participant gain an understanding of weight transfer, shifting to different parts of the body, as well as development of balance. Contrasting cue words can be used to vary the quality of movement that the body is capable of. The following action words help the participant understand the types of movements their body is capable of.

stretch	....	collapse
sharp	....	smooth
slither	....	slink
twist	....	reach

Other simple instructions to help develop body awareness include: *move your hand by itself, move one hand and one leg only* or *support your weight on two body parts, on three body parts.*

Developing an internal sense of how the body moves, referred to by Gardner as *bodily-kinaesthetic intelligence*(Gardner, 1993), is effectively developed through creative movement. Understanding the limitations of the body and the way in which it moves, and being able to master its movements, leads to a positive self-image, which in turn leads to positive self-esteem.

Temporal Awareness

Temporal awareness is involved when a body part is isolated and moved quickly or slowly. Quality of movement affects its fluidity. For example, a movement can be graceful or jerky. Each of these qualitative words can be used to describe an action that is slow or quick. The whole self can be made to move with different temporal qualities. "Movement occurs in a particular time as does music, sometimes with rhythm patterns or beats, always with a certain length or duration, and with slow, moderate, or fast tempo" (Zukowski and Dickson, p. 8). Ordering and sequencing of movements and combining them to create a pattern are further components in the development of temporal awareness through creative movement. Sometimes one move is given a particular accent and children may be instructed to emphasize one movement in the sequence they have created.

Temporal awareness includes *flow* or *quality* of a movement as it affects the timing of a movement. For example, an action can be sustained or jerky. An action can be carried out quickly or in slow motion, as a movie reduced to half speed. Children may be asked to combine various speeds of movement so that one action is sustained while the other is carried out very quickly. Often contrasting descriptor words are used to affect the quality of movement. Some examples include:

float down, like
a leaf from a tree .... *crash like an icicle*
melt .... *collapse*
fast .... *slow*
sustained .... *sudden*

In developing your own set of key words, look for ones that offer a contrast of energetic and relaxed movement qualities as well as different pacing in the movements.

THE GOALS AND BENEFITS OF CREATIVE MOVEMENT

Creative movement is used as an "educational vehicle for children to extend their movement vocabulary, increase physical skills, improve and maintain all components of physical fitness, and learn about themselves and others"(CAPHER, 1988, p.3). This goal, presented by the Canadian Association of Physical Education, Health, and Recreation (CAPHER) clearly sets the tone to identify the benefits.

Creative movement is enjoyed both for its outward expression of the self and the visual pleasure it gives those watching. It is a means of interpreting feelings, sounds, and/or words through individual self expression. This form of movement develops a sense of pleasure achieved through kinaesthetic actions.

Creative movement and dance offer movement with less structured or rigid rules than conventional dance forms. There is no right or wrong way to carry out an action. It is open-ended and nonthreatening, both to the child and the educator. For this reason, a creative movement program is adaptable to working with a varied developmental level. We have found that this form of movement education lends itself well to integrating intellectually and physically challenged children. Direction is provided by the educator and there is room for varied interpretation. The product is variable and important but it is the process that is emphasized. There is tremendous opportunity for children to express themselves in their own way.

Creative movements successfully combine perceptual components with fundamental movement skills. You will be able to provide children with opportunities to explore the potentials of their body through locomotor, nonlocomotor, and manipulative skills.

Rhythm and movement can act as catalysts, transferring experiences learned through the senses to the mind (Aldrich, 1989). Through perceptual motor experiences, motor skills, balance, and fitness are developed simultaneous to the enhancement of cognitive and affective abilities (CAPHER, 1988).

BEGINNING YOUR CREATIVE MOVEMENT SESSION

We have introduced creative movement with children as young as three years old. In the early years, movement expression is limited to exploring basic fundamental locomotor and nonlocomotor skills. Sometimes the addition of a prop,such as a light -weight scarf will add an interesting dimension to the movement while simultaneously enhancing manipulative skills. These manipulative skills are only secondary to the movement and do not provide the focal point. The first concepts we introduce consist of simple body and spatial awareness. When the children are about four years of age we begin to introduce the concepts of directional and temporal awareness. When they are five and six, creative movement is used as a vehicle for expression of inner feelings. We ask children to show us how they walk when they are happy, tired, or in a rush. When they are six, we begin to introduce combinations of movement patterns, turning creative movement into creative dance. The addition of self-expression through movement is an important one. By watching children's interpretation of feelings through movement, you will be able to learn a great deal about how they feel and what they think. In general, the way in which we move our bodies can be influenced by cultural context.

In creative movement you can isolate body parts and focus on their range of movement. For example, reach up as high as you can using one arm, now swing that arm to the side, let it swing like a pendulum. You can also focus on the integration of some or all body parts and explore the synchronization and harmony that is possible through combinations of movements. This sounds like a contradiction, but it is not. Through this expressive form of movement, children can work on each body part separately, exploring their range of motion, and finally integrating all body parts into a movement story. By moving creatively, we encourage children to define their own space and understand the limits of their own bodies. Children enjoy watching other children move and this often stimulates their own movements. It is also aesthetically pleasing to watch creative movements and dance expression. In observing others move, children begin to appreciate the ways in which they can move their bodies and value the movement expression of others.

Questions such as *How does your body move through space. How do your body parts function? Can you run fast or walk slowly, can you jump high or crouch down low?* are but a few ideas that you and the children can explore together. It is through the creative movement program that you can successfully weave a curriculum of developmentally appropriate activities that include varied physical, motor, perceptual, emotional, and cognitive concepts. The provision of uninterrupted movement also promotes physical fitness in a nonthreatening environment.

All creative movement classes should begin with a warmup. Warmups are intended to set the tone and develop physical fitness by providing active movement sessions that elevate the heart rate. They are used to introduce the movement concept that will be worked on in a particular session. Usually warmup sessions use a lot of space and begin with simple directional cues. As you get into the main body of the class, more complex concepts of temporal and body awareness can be presented.

We would like to share a personal experience that should put you at ease if you are planning your first creative movement session.

♦♦♦

> *Gerry decided to introduce creative movement to his group of four year old children. He put on the tape of "La Bamba" which he knew had good rhythmic quality. He asked his children "How does this music make you feel? Would you like to move to the music?" Most of the children watched, some got up and moved, no one had any feelings about the music.*

♦♦

The experience was a disaster. Does this sound familiar? Let's examine what went wrong. Firstly, a child of four cannot be expected to express his feelings about music and move with passion the first time he hears a piece. Present the music and let the children explore movements without any set parameters. Secondly, rather than ask IF they would like to move, say: "Let's all move to the music." Using a positive directive will be much more effective than asking a question. Also, notice the word *let's*, it implies joining in. Model an appreciation of movement. This tells children that it is valuable and that you believe it. An educator watching from the sidelines promotes apathy.

Take time to encourage children's movements by providing praise where you can. Comment on the type of movement you are seeing. Say things like "I see you found an interesting way to walk around the room" or "I like your jumping idea." Help children acquire a sense of pride in their accomplishments. Help them individualize their movements. "Inhibitions are overcome and good feelings about self emerge as discovering, identifying, and accepting are encouraged" (Flemming, p. 5).

Provide children with enough time and opportunity to explore how their body moves. It is this exploration that will enable the children to develop an understanding about their movement potential. Creative movement is not about an end result. It is about the process of problem solving what the body is capable of doing. This information can then be transferred to many other motor skills throughout life. After all, directional and spatial cues are used in most ball handling sports, body and temporal awareness are strong components of gymnastics and swimming, and so on.

It is essential that you do not correct dance style. Creative movement is interpretive and there is no right or wrong way. In the preschool years, we should not be concerned with teaching dance technique as dance positions may be harmful to developing bones. For example, children should not be asked to stand in specific position or with a perfect ballet turnout.

Ask many open-ended questions to assist children in the discovery process. The Learning Opportunities at the end of this chapter are meant to provide a few ideas about how you can get started. We rely on everyday situations that children can easily relate to as our main source of ideas for creative movement expression.

Take creative movement outdoors when you can. Even in winter, clad in snowsuits, creative movement provides an excellent opportunity for fun and learning. Creative movement can also be used as a means of warming up before exploring large stationary equipment outdoors. Movement qualities will vary when performed on a mound of snow as opposed to being carried out on a gym floor. Clad in snowsuits, the range of motion will change and children will need to adapt to this different feeling.

Music and percussion instruments are effective tools to help provide beat and rhythm. Good forms of music include show music, popular and modern, classical, electronic and synthesized music and sounds, as well as 20th century and New Age music. Some New Age music composers include *Vangelis, John Williams, and Phillip Glass.* There are many others that you might be familiar with.

The child does not have to perform a specific dance or exercise and the educator does not need a dance background to successfully carry out a creative movement session. It is not essential that you have any high level of technique in delivering this type of experience. As an educator, the most important skill you need in leading a successful creative movement session is ENTHUSIASM. Use the Learning Opportunities provided, modify them, or create your own, and begin.

RELATIONSHIPS

Creative movements can be carried out individually. Each person develops his own actions in relation to available space. He explores movements of body parts in relation to each other. He must be aware of others in the room in order not to infringe on the personal space of another child or participant,

These movements can also be carried out in partners. Participants can match actions, contrast them, follow, or mirror. They develop a sensitivity to each other's movements and style of moving. They learn to support and assist each other in movement experiences.

Three or more participants can group together to carry out a series of actions. Creative dance emerges when a group carries out isolated creative movements and joins them together. With a group carrying out these movements together many considerations about the formation of the group must be taken into consideration. They look at group position and group shape. The group can be in a straight line, circle, scattered, or together.

Relationships help develop sensitivity to and respect for others. As in nonelimination games, there is cooperation and partner and group decision making. In group work there is the development of leadership and fellowship roles(CAPHER, 1988).

GUIDED FANTASY

Guided fantasies are used for relaxation. They help develop imagery and a greater understanding of one's own body. "Before we establish language, we visualize pictures in our minds and link them to concepts"(Margulies, p.6). Guided fantasies help bring us back in touch with the pictures in our mind. Too often, this area of development is neglected and we forget how to conjure important images and pictures. Guided fantasies are often neglected as a part of a comprehensive psychomotor program. They are a valuable means of helping older children come in touch with their minds and bodies. In general, we do not suggest introducing guided fantasies before the age of five. Our experiences have found them to be most useful with kindergarten and schoolage children.

Guided fantasies can be simple, where children are encouraged to sit quietly for a moment and reflect on a favourite part of the day, or they may involve complex imagery such as some of the Learning Opportunities provided below. We have seen guided fantasies used successfully in extended day programming for school age children as a means of relaxation. Guided fantasy is what Murdock describes as an effective means of developing intrapersonal intelligence (Murdock, 1987).   Guided fantasies also serve as a vehicle to bring one's mind in touch with one's body, to develop a heightened awareness of one's physical and inner self. Sometimes we may have difficulty expressing certain concepts that can be visualized internally. Guided fantasy can help give context or meaning to thoughts and movements.

IMAGERY

Imagery provides a large part of the impetus for movement. It is also used in guided fantasy. In movement we do not see the thought process but the product of imagery. In guided fantasy, the imagery is private and belongs only to each individual who sees the thought or action in his mind. Sometimes, discussions following a guided fantasy session can be used to learn more about the children you are working with. It is also a vehicle to articulate images and feelings that the participant has.

You can provide children with cues that will enhance movement potential. For example, it is imagery that is used when you say, "Fly like your favourite bird." You can be fairly certain that the children will have some understanding of what we mean and that by using images in their own minds they will either fly with arms outstretched like a large bird or waddle like Sesame Street's Big Bird.

Imagery needs to be developmentally and culturally appropriate, selecting words and concepts that the individual can bring to mind. Hankin (1992) cautions us not to misuse imagery. Cues that are too restrictive are no different than asking questions that have single answers. Stay away from selected theme oriented movement. For example, if you tell a child to move like a frog, you will most likely get a lot of hopping that looks rather the same. Children will hop up and crouch down, all moving in the same direction, probably with a lot of accompanying ribbit-like sound effects. Rather, Hankin suggests focusing on the movement qualities such as, "let me see how your frog rests on the bank of the river and prepares to get the insect in the water for lunch." This will elicit a much more creative movement response, encouraging high hopping, far hopping, quick darting hops, and slow calculated hops, depending on the interpretation each child gives to the movement story. Some frogs will hop cautiously while others will produce sudden, quick actions. Your choice of words will affect the quality of movement.

Cognitive skills are developed through the use of imagery as the child links mind and body with imagination and information processing. The image conjured in the dancer's mind is what produces the movement outcome. We can never see what goes on in the dancer's mind, we can only see the product of his movement, which is the product of his thinking. Imagery is often used as a way for the educator to get the children to visualize an experience before carrying it out. It provides each mover with a unique interpretation of the message that is being communicated.

CHAPTER HIGHLIGHTS

This chapter ties together the many concepts presented throughout this book. Creative movement is used a a vehicule for self expression. It invovles perceptual and motor experiences. Creative movement usually relies on individual movmements of whole group participation. Sometimes, partners or small groups are formed to change the dynamics and movement experiences. This form of movement provides excellent opportunities to develop skills involving balance and exploration of the body's range of motion.

Guided fantasy and imagery are internal expressions where perceptual and motor experiences occur in the mind's eye.

In conclusion, both creative movement and guided fantasy bring together the full range of perceptual and cognitive elements. While these forms of learning do not focus on traditional linear teaching methods, their value for the kinaesthetic or intuitive learner is limitless. They help us relax and be attentive to the rhythm of our own body. In a world where children are pressured to achieve, succeed, rush from one activity to another, creative movement and guided fantasy serve as an excellent means for the individual to gain full understanding and control of his own body and what its capacity for movement is.

Creative movement and guided fantasy support the notion that mind and body are connected (Aldrich, 1989).

LEARNING OPPORTUNITIES

1. ‖   <u>Melt</u>

    Age: five years and up

    Ratio: one to many

    Procedure:

    Tell the following story to the children. "Brrrr, it is cold today. I woke up and there was frost on the ground. I left some water outside and it froze like a solid block of ice." *Ask the children to show you what shape their water froze in.*

    "As the sun rose higher in the sky, The water began to melt, at first very slowly. It melted down into a big puddle on the floor." *Encourage the children to melt drip by drip until they are a puddle spread all over the floor.*

    "All the water melted together and the little puddles everywhere spread out until they were all attached into one big, huge puddle." *Repeat key words as needed to expand movement potential and imagery.*

    At age seven introduce new science concepts. "At high noon the sun was very strong and the puddle began to evaporate, rising into the clouds. This took a very long time until all the water reached the sky. The very next day, the clouds were so full, that the water came down in light rain drops, bouncing on the ground."

    We suggest that you link books and science experiments to some of the concepts presented here. Creative movements become the thread that weaves a number of cognitive concepts.

    focus: auditory awareness, body awareness, nonlocomotor movements, imagery

2. ‖ <u>Take a Walk on the Wide Side</u>

Age: three years and up

Ratio: one to many

Procedure:

Exploring locomotor concepts. Ask children to walk with very wide steps, very narrow steps, high on their toes, with knees bent. Ask them to think of an animal that they like and to walk like that animal. Try and guess what animal the children are. Have them pretend to be that animal looking for something to drink.

focus: locomotor movements, auditory awareness, spatial awareness

3. ‖ <u>Stop and Go</u>

Age: two and a half to six years

Ratio: one to many

Procedure:

Introduce a tambourine or drum. Recall the "going" and "stopping" sound from Chapter 2. On the "going" sound, have children find any way of travelling around the room creating pathways on the floor. On the "stopping" sound, children freeze on the spot. Provide a slow, deliberate tapping sound to encourage slow walking with high steps. Now run your fingers around the skin of the instrument to create a scraping sound. Usually children will begin to slither and crawl to this sound. Now provide a quick tempo rat-a-tat- tat to encourage the children to move quickly around the room. Strike the "stop" sound between each action. Talk about all the different ways that children can freeze. Encourage children to change directions often while travelling around the room and to make interesting patterns on the floor as they move about.

focus: locomotor movements, auditory awareness, spatial awareness, directional awareness

4. ‖ <u>Attached</u>

Age: three to eight years

Ratio: one to many

Procedure:

Beat the drum for four counts. On 1, 2, 3, 4, ask the children to attach themselves to a partner and make a shape together with that partner. Have the children hold the shape for a while, then repeat the drum count. Tell the children on 4, to find a new partner to create a shape with.

Variation # 1

When the children create a shape, tell them to arrange themselves so that one partner is very high and one is very low. Have them move again to the drum beat, this time when they connect have one partner very wide and one very thin. (Adapted from Zukowski and Dickson, 1990)

focus: auditory awareness, nonelimination, locomotor movements, cooperation

5. ‖ <u>Mirrors and Shadows</u>

Age: four to twelve years

Ratio: partner activity

Procedure:

Have children paired together. One child leads the actions while the other provides the mirror image. Tell the leader to move very slowly so that his mirror can follow. The first time, have children try any slow move with the mirror copying. Then, ask the lead child to act what he does in the morning when he gets up.

Variation # 1

Repeat the same procedure, only this time one child is the lead, while the other is the shadow. Talk with the children about the differences between the way our mirror image moves and the way that our shadow moves.

focus: cooperation, nonelimination, nonlocomotor movements, locomotor movements, spatial awareness

6. ‖ <u>Splish, Splat</u>

    Age: three tp eight years

    Ratio: one to many

Procedure:

Use simple words to elicit movement qualities and develop vocabulary. Here are a list of a few descriptive words:
        Splat, Splish
        Float, Flit, Fly
        Bounce, Jump, Rebound
        Melt, Drip, Plunk
        Slither, Slide, Creep, Crawl

focus: locomotor movements, nonelimination, imagery

7. ‖ <u>Mountain View</u>

    Age: six years and up

    Ratio: one to many

Procedure:

Imagine you are standing at the base of the mountain. Look up.....look way up.....look way, way up. What do you see? (Leave a few seconds for the children to create an image in their mind.) Begin slowly walking up the mountain. (Pause for five to ten seconds.) Stop for a minute, take a deep breath. Turn and look behind you to see how far you have come. Now look back up. How much farther do you have to go? You can do it. Begin again to walk up the mountain until you reach the very top of the mountain.

Once at the top, stop. Sit down and relax. Take a deep breath and look around. Take lots of time to see what is all around. How does it feel to be sitting up here way at the top of the mountain? Relax, take one last deep breath. We are now going to head down the mountain. Run down the mountain. Run...run...run all the way down. You have made it. You are back where you started. Catch your breath and relax.

focus: imagery, auditory awareness

8. ‖ <u>Wishing Star</u>

Age: five years and up

Ratio: one to many

Procedure:

Have each of the children lie on his back. Dim the lights in the room. Play New Age music or soft Oriental music in the background. Speak in a low, soft mellow voice and say:

"Everyone stare at the ceiling. Take a deep, quiet breath. Breathe in. Breathe out. Feel your breathing getting slower. If you wish , you may close your eyes. Now, imagine you can see a star. It is your very favourite star. It belongs to you and to no one else. This is your special wishing star. On this star you are safe from the world. Now that you are on this star, you can imagine you are any place you want. Take yourself to your favourite place. Imagine how it feels. Is it warm in your favourite place? You feel very safe. Take a deep breath. What does the air smell like in your favourite place?"

Give the children 30 seconds to think about their place. While they are doing this play New Age music to help set the tone. Once 30 seconds have passed, tell the children: "It is now time to leave your special star. Breathe in deeply, open your eyes, and come back to the classroom." Give them a few minutes to come back to reality. You may ask them to tell you about their place, but remember, it must be their decision.

focus: imagery, auditory awareness

REFERENCES

Aldrich, Kenneth R. (1989) "Rhythm, Movement, and Synchrony, Effective Teaching Tools", *Journal Of Physical Education Recreation and Dance*. April, 91-94.

Flemming, Gladys Andrews (1976) *Creative Rhythmic Movement, Boys and Girls Dancing.* Englewood-Cliffs, N.J.: Prentice-Hall Inc.

Gerhardt, Lydia A. (1973) *Moving and Knowing, The Young Child Orients Himself in Space.* Englewood-Cliffs, N.J.: Prentice-Hall, Inc.

Gardner, Howard (1993) *Frames of Mind.* Anniversary edition, New York: Basic Books.

Hankin, Toby (1992) "Presenting Creative Dance Activities to Children: Guidelines for the Nondancer, *Journal of Physical Education Recreation and Dance*, 22-24 , Feb.

Jenkins, Mary A. (1983) "Composing and Guiding Creative Movement, *Journal of Physical Education Recreation and Dance*, January, p.85-87.

Lord, Madeleine and Bruneau, Monik (1983) *La Parole Est A La Danse*, Sainte-Foy, Quebec: Les Editions La Liberte

Margulies, Nancy (1991) *Mapping Inner Space*. Tuscon, Arizona: Zephyr Press.

Murdock, Maureen (1987) *Spinning Inward, Using Guided Imagery With Children for Learning, Creativity and Relaxation*, Boston, Mass: Shambalah Publications Inc.

Thorton, S. (1971) *A Movement Perspective of Rudolph Laban*. London: Macdonald and Evans Limited.

Zukowski, Ginger and Dickson, Ardie (1990) *On The Move, A Handbook For Exploring Creative Movement With Young Children*, Carbondale and Edwardsville: Southern Illinois University Press.

APPENDIX A

---

*Developmentally Appropriate Physical Education for Children**

As we enter the 21st century the importance and value of regular physical activity has been recognized as never before. Accompanying this recognition is the awareness that childhood is the time to begin the development of active and healthy lifestyles.

Children do not automatically develop the skills, knowledge, attitudes, and behaviours that lead to regular and enjoyable participation in physical activity. They must be taught. The responsibility for this instruction is vested primarily in physical education programs in the schools.

In recent years a growing body of research, theory, and practical experience has sharpened our understanding about the beneficial aspects of physical education programs for children - and those that are counterproductive. The purpose of this document is to describe, in a very straight-forward way, practices that are both appropriate and inappropriate for children in preschool and elementary school physical education programs.

Quality Physical Education for Children

The Council of Physical Education for Children (COPEC), the nation's largest professional association of children's physical education teachers, believes that quality, daily physical education should be available to all children. Quality physical education is developmen-

tally appropriate for children. "Developmentally appropriate programs are both age appropriate and individually appropriate; that is, the program is designed for the age group served and implemented with attention to the needs and differences of the individual children enroled" (NAEYC, 1986). The outcome of a developmentally appropriate program of physical education is an individual who is "physically educated."

In 1990, the National Association for Sport and Physical Education (NASPE) defined a physically educated person as one who:

· HAS learned the skills necessary to perform a variety of physical activities
· DOES participate regularly in physical activity
· IS physically fit
· KNOWS the implications of and the benefits from involvement in physical activities
· VALUES physical activity and its contributions to a healthful lifestyle

Developmentally appropriate physical education programs for children provide an important first step towards becoming a physically educated person.

Premises of Physical Education Programs for Children

In any discussion of physical education programs for children there are three major premises that need to be understood.

Reprinted from "Developmentally Appropriate Physical Education for Children" with permission of the National Association for Sport and Physical Education, 1900 Association Drive, Reston, VA 22091

1. Physical education and athletic programs have different purposes.

   Athletic programs are essentially designed for youngsters who are eager to specialize in one or more sports and refine their talents in order to compete with others of similar interests and abilities. Developmentally appropriate physical education programs, in contrast, are designed for every child - from the physically gifted to the physically challenged. The intent is to provide children of all abilities and interest with a foundation of movement experiences that will eventually lead to active and healthy lifestyles - athletic competition may be one part of this lifestyle, but is not the only part.

2. Children are not miniature adults.

   Children have very different abilities, needs, and interests than adults. It is inadequate to simply "water down" adult sport or activity programs and assume that they will be beneficial. Children need, and learn from, programs that are designed specifically with their needs and differences in mind.

3. Children in school today will not be adults in today's world.

   More than ever before we are in a time of rapid change. Consequently, educators have the challenge of preparing children to live as adults in a world that has yet to be clearly defined and understood. The only certainty is that they will have different opportunities and interest than currently exist. Contemporary programs introduce children to the world of today, while also preparing them to live in the uncertain world of tomorrow. In brief, they help them learn how to learn - and to enjoy the process of discovering and exploring new and different challenges in the physical domain.
   Tomorrow's physical activities may look quite different from today's. Present programs need to prepare children with basic movement skills that can be used in any activity, whether it be popular today or one yet to be invented. Mastery of basic skills encourages the development and refinement of more complex skills leading to the ultimate enjoyment of physical activity for its own sake.

Intended Audience

This document is written for teachers, parents, school administrators, policy makers, and other individuals who are responsible for the physical education of children. It is intended to provide specific guidelines that will help them recognize practices that are in the best interests of children (developmentally appropriate) and those that are counterproductive, or even harmful (developmentally inappropriate). It needs to be understood that the components described in this appendix are, in actuality, interrelated. They are separated here only for purposes of clarity and ease of reading. It should also be understood that these components are not all-inclusive. They do represent, however, most of the characteristics of developmentally appropriate programs of physical education for children.

Appropriate and Inappropriate Physical Education Practices

Component: Curriculum

Appropriate Practice

- The physical education curriculum has an obvious scope and sequence based on goals and objectives that are beneficial for all children. It includes a balance of skills, concepts, games, educational gymnastics, rhythms, and dance experiences designed to enhance the cognitive, motor, affective, and physical fitness development of every child.

Inappropriate Practice

The physical education curriculum lacks developed goals and objectives and is based primarily upon the teacher's interests, preferences, and background rather than those of the children. For example, the curriculum consists primarily of large group games.

Component: Development of Movement Concepts and Motor Skills

Appropriate Practice

- Children are provided with plenty of worthwhile practice opportunities which enable them to develop a functional understanding of movement concepts (body awareness, space awareness, effort, and relationships) and build competence and confidence in their ability to perform a variety of motor skills (locomotor, non-locomotor, and manipulative).

Inappropriate Practice

- Children participate in a limited number of games and activities where the opportunity for individual children to develop basic concepts and motor skills is restricted.

Component: Cognitive Development

Appropriate Practice

- Physical education activities are designed with both the physical and the cognitive development of children in mind.

- Experiences which encourage children to question, integrate, analyze, communicate, and apply cognitive concepts, as well as gain a multi-cultural view of the world are provided, thus making physical education a part of the total educational experience.

Inappropriate Practice

- The unique role of physical education, which allows children to learn to move while also moving to learn, is not explored and recognized by instructors.
- Children do not receive opportunities to integrate their physical education experience with art, music, and other classroom experience.

Component: Affective Development

Appropriate Practice

- Teachers intentionally design and teach activities throughout the year which allow children the opportunity to work together for the purpose of improving their social and cooperation skills. These activities also help children develop a positive self-concept.
- Teachers help children experience and feel the satisfaction and joy which results from regular participation in physical activity.

Inappropriate Practice

- Teachers fail to intentionally enhance the affective development of children when activities are excluded which foster the development of cooperation and social skills.
- Teachers ignore opportunities to help children understand the emotions they feel as a result of participation in physical activity.

Component: Concepts of Fitness

Appropriate Practice

· Children participate in activities that are designed to help them understand and value the important concepts of physical fitness and the contribution they make to a healthy lifestyle.

Inappropriate Practice

· Children are required to participate in fitness activities, but are not helped to understand the reasons why.

Component: Physical Fitness Tests

Appropriate Practice

· Physical fitness tests are used as part of the ongoing process of helping children understand, enjoy, improve, and/or maintain their physical health and well-being.
· Test results are shared privately with children and their parents as a tool for developing their physical fitness knowledge, understanding, and competence.
· As part of an ongoing program of physical education, children are physically prepared so they can safely complete each component of a physical test battery.

Inappropriate Practice

· Physical fitness tests are given once or twice a year solely for the purpose of qualifying children for awards or because they are required by a school district or state department.
· Children are required to complete a physical fitness test battery without understanding why they are performing the

tests or the implications of their individual results as they apply to their future health and well-being.
· Children are required to take physical fitness tests without adequate conditioning (e.g., students are made to run a mile after "practising" it only one day the week before).

Component: Calisthenics

Appropriate Practice

· Appropriate exercises are taught for the specific purpose of improving the skill, coordination, and/or fitness levels of children.
· Children are taught exercises that keep the body in proper alignment, thereby allowing the muscles to lengthen without placing stress and strain on the surrounding joints, ligaments, and tendons (e.g., the sitting toe touch).

Inappropriate Practice

· Children perform standardized calisthenics with no specific purpose in mind (e.g., jumping jacks, windmills, toe touches).
· Exercises are taught which compromise body alignment and place unnecessary stress on the joints and muscles (e.g., deep-knee bends, ballistic [bouncing] stretches, and standing straight-legged toe touches).

Component: Fitness as Punishment

Appropriate Practice

. Fitness activities are used to help children increase their physical fitness levels in a supportive, motivating, and progressive manner, thereby promoting positive lifetime fitness attitudes.

Inappropriate Practice

- Physical fitness activities are used by teachers as punishment for children's misbehaviour (e.g., students running laps, or doing push-ups, because they are off-task or slow to respond to teacher instruction).

Component: Assessment

Appropriate Practice

- Teacher discussions are based primarily on ongoing assessments of children as they participate in physical education class activities (formative evaluation), and not on the basis of a single test score (summative evaluation).
- Assessment of children's physical progress and achievement is used to individualize instruction, plan yearly curriculum and weekly lessons, identify children with special needs, communicate with parents, and evaluate the program's effectiveness.

Inappropriate Practice

- Children are evaluated on the basis of fitness test score or on a single physical skill test. For example, children receive a grade in physical education based on their scores on a standardized fitness test or on the number of times they can continuously jump rope.

Component: Regular Involvement for Every Child

Appropriate Practice

- Children participate in their regularly scheduled physical education class because it is recognized as an important part of their overall education.

Inappropriate Practice

- Children are removed from physical education classes to participate in classroom activities and/or as a punishment for not completing assignments, or for misbehaviour in the classroom.

Component: Active Participation for Every Child

Appropriate Practice

- *All* children are involved in activities which allow them to remain continuously active.
- Classes are designed to meet a child's need for active participation in all learning experiences.

Inappropriate Practice

- Activity time is limited because children are waiting in lines for a turn in relay races, to be chosen for a team, or due to limited equipment or playing games such as Duck, Duck, Goose.
- Children are organized into large groups where getting a turn is based on individual competitiveness or aggressive behaviour.
- Children are eliminated with no chance to re-enter the activity, or they must sit for long periods of time. For example, activities such as musical chairs, dodgeball, and elimination tag provide limited opportunities for many children, especially the slower, less agile ones who actually need activity the most.

Component: Dance/Rhythmical Experiences

Appropriate Practice

· The physical education curriculum includes a variety of rhythmical, expressive, and dance experiences designed with the physical, cultural, emotional, and social abilities of the children in mind.

Inappropriate Practice

· The physical education curriculum included no rhythmical, expressive, or cultural dance experiences for children.

· Folk and square dances (designed for adults) are taught too early or to the exclusion of other dance forms in the curriculum or are not modified to meet the developmental needs of the children.

Component: Educational Gymnastics

Appropriate Practice

· Children are encouraged to develop skills appropriate to their ability and confidence levels in non-competitive situations centering around the broad skill areas of balancing, rolling, jumping and landing, and weight transfer.
· Children are able to practice on apparatus designed for their confidence and skill level, and can design sequences which allow for success at their personal skill level.

Inappropriate Practice

· All students are expected to perform predetermined stunts and routines on and off apparatus, regardless of their skill level, body composition, and level of confidence.
· Routines are competitive, are the sole basis for a grade, and/or must be per-formed solo while the remainder of the class sits and watches.

Component: Rules Governing Game Play

Appropriate Practice

· Teachers and/or children modify official rules, regulations, equipment, and playing space of adult sports to match the varying abilities of the children.

Inappropriate Practice

· Official, adult rules of team sports govern the activities in physical education classes, resulting in low rates of success and lack of enjoyment for many children.

Component: Forming Teams

Appropriate Practice

· Teams are formed in ways that preserve the dignity and self-respect of every child. For example, teacher privately forms teams by using knowledge of children's skill abilities or the children form teams cooperatively or randomly.

Inappropriate Practice

· Teams are formed by "captains" publicly selecting one child at a time, thereby exposing the lower-skilled children to peer ridicule.
· Teams are formed by pitting "boys against the girls," thereby emphasizing gender

differences rather than cooperation and working together.

Component: Gender-Directed Activities

Appropriate Practice

· Girls and boys are provided equal access to participation in individual, partner, small group, and team activities. Both girls and boys are equally encouraged, supported, and socialized towards successful achievement in all realms of physical activities.
· Statements by physical education teachers support leadership opportunities and provide positive reinforcement in a variety of activities which may be considered gender-neutral.

Inappropriate Practice

· Girls are encouraged to participate in activities which stress traditionally feminine roles, whereas boys are encouraged to participate in more aggressive activities.
· Boys are more often provided with leadership roles in physical education class. Statements by physical education teachers reinforce traditional socialization patterns which provide for greater and more aggressive participation by boys and lesser and more passive participation by girls.

Component: Number of Children on a Team

Appropriate Practice

· Children participate in team games (e.g., 2-3 per team), which allow for numerous practice opportunities while also allowing

them to learn about the various aspects of the game being taught.

Inappropriate Practice

· Children participate in full sided games (e.g., the class of 30 is split into two teams of 15 and these two teams play each other) thereby leading to few practice opportunities.

Component: Competition

Appropriate Practice

· Activities emphasize self-improvement, participation, and cooperation instead of winning and losing.
· Teachers are aware of the nature of competition and do not *require* higher levels of competition from children before they are ready. For example, children are allowed to choose between a game in which score is kept and one that is just for practice.

Inappropriate Practice

· Children are *required* to participate in activities that label children as "winners" and "losers."
· Children are *required* to participate in activities that compare one child's or team's performance against others (e.g., a race in which the winning child or team is clearly identified).

Component: Success Rate

Appropriate Practice

· Children are given the opportunity to practice skills at high rates of success adjusted for their individual skill levels.

Inappropriate Practice

· Children are asked to perform activities which are too easy or too hard, causing frustration, boredom, and/or misbe-haviour.
· All children are expected to perform to the same standards without allowing for individual abilities and interests.

Component: Class Size

Appropriate Practice

· Physical education classes contain the same number of children as the classroom (e.g., 25 children per class).

Inappropriate Practice

· Children participate in a physical education class which includes more children than the classroom. (For example, two or more classrooms are placed with one certified teacher and one or more teacher aides.)

Component: Days per Week/Length of Class Time

Appropriate Practice

· Children are given the opportunity to participate daily in scheduled, instructional physical education throughout the year, exclusive of recess.
· Length of class is appropriate for the developmental level of the children.

Inappropriate Practice

· Children do not receive daily, instructional physical education.
· Children's age and maturational levels are not taken into account when physical education schedules are developed.

Component: Facilities

Appropriate Practice

· Children are provided an environment in which they have adequate space to move freely and safely. Both inside and outside areas are provided so that classes need not be cancelled, or movement severely limited, because of inclement weather.

Inappropriate Practice

· Physical education classes are regularly held in a school hallway or in a classroom thereby restricting opportunities to move freely and without obstructions.

Component: Equipment

Appropriate Practice

· Enough equipment is available so that each child benefits from maximum participation. For example, every child in a class would have a ball.
· Equipment is matched to the size, confidence, and skill level of the children so that they are motivated to actively participate in physical education classes.

Inappropriate Practice

· An insufficient amount of equipment is available for the number of children in a class (e.g., one ball for every four children).
· Regulation or "adult size" equipment is used which may inhibit skill development, injure, or intimidate the children.

Component: PE and Recess

Appropriate Practice

· Physical education classes are planned and organized to provide children with opportunities to acquire the physical, emotional, cognitive, and social benefits of physical education.

Inappropriate Practice

· "Free-play," or recess, is used as a *substitute* for daily, organized physical education lessons. Free-play, in this case, is characterized by lack of goals, organization, planning, and instruction.

Component: Field Days

Appropriate Practice

· The field day, if offered, is designed so that every child is a full participant and derives a feeling of satisfaction and joy from a festival of physical activity.
· Opportunities are provided for children to voluntarily choose from a variety of activities that are intended purely for enjoyment.

Inappropriate Practice

· Field days, if offered, are designed so that there is intense team, group, or individual competition with winners and losers clearly identified.
· One or two children are picked to represent an entire class, thereby reducing others to the role of spectator.

APPENDIX B

LEARNING OPPORTUNITY TABLE

This appendix is provided to assist you in the planning and preparation of a developmentally appropriate curriculum. All learning opportunities were designed based on the concepts and ideas provided throughout htis book as well as those ideas put forth in Appendix A. We consider criteria that includes: ensuring that there is enough equipment for all children, that opportunities cater to whole group participation and inclusion rather than exclusion, and that opportunities enhance physical fitness. We strive to provide opportunities that are presented in a motivating format and "promote positive lifetime fitness attitudes" (Sanders, 1992, p.126). Opportunities using apparatus are designed and presented to accommodate variable skill level within a group. There are opportunities that improve balance and body alignment. There are a variety of indoor as well as outdoor opportunities to choose from.

We have taken all the learning opportunities throughout the book and listed them in alphabetical order. They are then identified by age, perceptual motor area, fundamental skill focus, physical fitness, balance, and nonelimination. A key is provided on the next page to assist you in using this table. We suggest using this table in the following way:

1. Identify the developmental stage you are working with. Look down the first set of columns and select from among the activities that correspond to the appropriate group.

2. Determine if you wish to develop fundamental skills, perceptual motor skills, balance, or physical fitness. Look down the appropriate columns to assist in your selection of learning opportunities. You will notice that almost all opportunities are non elimination, in accordance with our philosophical approach to early childhood education.

3. Look down the last column to find the page that describes the desired activity choice(s).

This table should assist you in planning a developmentally appropriate curriculum for many years to come. We have provided two spaces at the end of the table for you to add two of your favourite activities.

The initials at the top of each page identify the age, area of motor skill, the perceptual area, whether an opportunity develops balance or physical fitness, and finally if it is a nonelimination activity. The key below will tell you what each initial stands for and is intended to assist you in using the table.

IT	infant/toddler	BA	body awareness
PS	preschool	SA	spatial awareness
SC	schoolage	DA	directional awareness
		FA	temporal awareness
LS	locomotor skills		
NL	nonlocomotor skills	BL	balance
MS	manipulative skills	PF	physical fitness
		NE	non elimination
VP	visual perception	Pg.	page
AP	auditory perception		
TP	tactile perception		

LEARNING OPPORTUNITIES	DEV'T STAGE			FUNDAMENTAL SKILLS			PERCEPTUAL MOTOR AREA							OTHER			Pg.
	IT	PS	SC	LS	NL	MS	VP	AP	TP	BA	SA	DA	TA	BL	PF	NE	
A climbing we will go	■			♦							★						73
Action Ball		■	■			♦						★		♥		♥	53
Alligator game		■	■	♦		♦	★									♥	178
Attached		■	■	♦				★								♥	197
Back to back		■	■		♦					★						♥	33
Balance board		■	■									★					31
Ball roll	■					♦	★				★	★					26
Boat out at sea	■	■	■			♦	★									♥	177
Bubble tag		■	■	♦											♥	♥	155
Cat and Mouse		■	■	♦		♦	★				★				♥	♥	179
Changing Places		■	■	♦		♦	★				★				♥	♥	177
Chase		■	■	♦										♥	♥	♥	51

LEARNING OPPORTUNITIES	DEV'T STAGE			FUNDAMENTAL SKILLS			PERCEPTUAL MOTOR AREA								OTHER		Pg.
	IT	PS	SC	LS	NL	MS	VP	AP	TP	BA	SA	DA	TA	BL	PF	NE	
Circle avoid ball			■			♦						★					♥	122
Circle untangle		■	■		♦	♦				★	★	★					♥	159
Climbing over the mountain		■	■	♦		♦	★				★						♥	179
Connected		■	■			♦						★					♥	175
Cooperative balls		■	■			♦											♥	176
Cooperative hot potato		■	■			♦	★	★				★					♥	152
Crazy carpets		■	■	♦								★				♥	♥	51
Crows and cranes		■	■	♦				★	★								♥	158
Exploration		■			♦		★	★	★		★	★					♥	174
Feel that beat	■	■			♦	♦		★	★								♥	25
Feely box	■	■	■			♦							★				♥	26
Five little monkeys		■		♦							★						♥	89

LEARNING OPPORTUNITIES	DEV'T STAGE			FUNDAMENTAL SKILLS			PERCEPTUAL MOTOR AREA							OTHER			Pg.
	IT	PS	SC	LS	NL	MS	VP	AP	TP	BA	SA	DA	TA	BL	PF	NE	
Freeze tag		■	■	♦										♥		♥	52
Head and shoulders	■	■			♦			★		★						♥	25
Hello song		■	■	♦				★								♥	139
Hokey Pokey		■	■		♦			★		★						♥	28
Hoops			■			♦						★				♥	122
Human machine			■		♦					★				♥		♥	33
Jump jump look who is in the box	■		■	♦												♥	72
Kick ball		■	■			♦	★					★		♥		♥	109
Kick that ball		■	■			♦	★		★			★		♥		♥	155
Kick time		■	■			♦	★		★					♥		♥	31
Let's throw		■	■			♦			★		★	★	★			♥	108
Lift off		■	■		♦										♥	♥	180

LEARNING OPPORTUNITIES	DEV'T STAGE			FUNDAMENTAL SKILLS			PERCEPTUAL MOTOR AREA							OTHER			Pg.
	IT	PS	SC	LS	NL	MS	VP	AP	TP	BA	SA	DA	TA	BL	PF	NE	
Little Peter rabbit		■				◆				★						♥	30
Little Tommy tittle mouse	■							★						♥		♥	71
Magic cloud		■	■			◆	★		★		★					♥	180
Magic tambourine		■	■	◆				★							♥	♥	195
Melt		■	■				★		★							♥	29
Mirroring		■	■	◆			★			★	★					♥	157
Mirrors and shadows		■	■	◆					★	★						♥	197
Modified frozen tag		■	■	◆		◆			★		★			♥	♥	♥	157
Mountain view		■	■				★	★								♥	198
Musical balance		■	■	◆	◆			★						♥	♥	♥	52
Musical hoops		■	■	◆	◆						★					♥	153
Newcomb ball		■	■			◆					★	★				♥	123

LEARNING OPPORTUNITIES	DEV'T STAGE			FUNDAMENTAL SKILLS			PERCEPTUAL MOTOR AREA							OTHER			Pg.
	IT	PS	SC	LS	NL	MS	VP	AP	TP	BA	SA	DA	TA	BL	PF	NE	
Objects		■				◆							★			♥	27
Partner pull-up		■	■	◆	◆					★				♥		♥	159
Person to person		■	■							★				♥		♥	32
Popcorn		■	■			◆	★								♥	♥	178
Potato sack hop			■	◆												♥	123
Quoits			■			◆					★	★				♥	110
Red light, green light		■		◆				★								♥	153
Red rover		■		◆				★								♥	156
Roll the ball		■				◆		★				★				♥	107
Row, row, row your boat	■	■			◆											♥	72
Sally says		■			◆					★						♥	30
Scarf dance		■	■			◆	★		★				★	♥		♥	173

LEARNING OPPORTUNITIES	DEV'T STAGE			FUNDAMENTAL SKILLS			PERCEPTUAL MOTOR AREA							OTHER			Pg.
	IT	PS	SC	LS	NL	MS	VP	AP	TP	BA	SA	DA	TA	BL	PF	NE	
Scarves		■				♦	★		★		★					♥	110
Sculptures in my garden			■			♦				★				♥		♥	90
Shake your sillies out		■			♦					★						♥	140
Snake		■	■	♦							★	★			♥	♥	90
Sound walk		■	■	♦				★								♥	34
Spaghetti arms		■	■		♦					★						♥	27
Splish, splash		■	■	♦	♦			★		★						♥	198
Spud		■	■			♦					★					♥	154
Squirrel		■	■			♦						★	★			♥	156
Statue game		■	■	♦	♦									♥		♥	89
Stiff as a board		■								★						♥	29
Stop and go		■		♦				★						♥		♥	197

LEARNING OPPORTUNITIES	DEV'T STAGE			FUNDAMENTAL SKILLS			PERCEPTUAL MOTOR AREA							OTHER			Pg.
	IT	PS	SC	LS	NL	MS	VP	AP	TP	BA	SA	DA	TA	BL	PF	NE	
Switch		■		◆			★	★			★	★				♥	160
Take a walk on the wide side		■	■	◆						★						♥	196
Target			■			◆	★					★				♥	121
Tenecoit			■			◆	★	★			★	★				♥	124
The Grand old Duke of York	■		■					★				★				♥	71
Twister	■	■	■							★				♥		♥	32
Tug boat	■	■				◆		★			★					♥	176
Up goes the castle		■	■		◆			★		★						♥	141
Wall ball		■	■			◆						★				♥	108
Water jumping			■	◆				★				★			♥	♥	90
Who lives there?		■				◆							★			♥	28
Wishing star			■				★									♥	199

LEARNING OPPORTUNITIES	DEV'T STAGE			FUNDAMENTAL SKILLS			PERCEPTUAL MOTOR AREA								OTHER		Pg.
	IT	PS	SC	LS	NL	MS	VP	AP	TP	BA	SA	DA	TA	BL	PF	NE	
Wrap around	■												★			♥	70
Zig zag		■		◆								★				♥	♥	33

APPENDIX C

RESOURCES

Parchutes can be purchased from:

Niagara Parchutes
P.O. Box 927
Niagara Falls, Ontario
Canada, L2E 6V8

(905) 358-5211

Parachute video available from:

DEVA Consultants
8 Minden Road
Montreal, Quebec
Canada, H3X 3M4

Fax (514) 342-0611

Sand toys, water toys, scissors and beads available from:

Wintergreen
519 North Rivermede Rd.
Concord, Ontario
Canada, L4K 3N1
Canada

GLOSSARY

auditory perception - perceiving the world through the sense of hearing.

automated response - when an action begins to occur spontaneously, without apparent premeditated thought. This usually happens only after many repetitions of the same task, through both practice and experience.

axial movements - these movements involve the use of the torso and limbs of the body and include such movements as twisting, bending and turning.

balance - maintaining equilibrium whether the centre of gravity stays in one place or is altered as the body moves.

base of support - refers to the parts of your body that are in contact with the floor or ground.

bilateral coordination - when children use their two hands together.

body awareness - involves a sense of self and a knowledge of the body parts and how they work.

body knowledge - cognitive understanding of body parts and how they function.

cardiovascular endurance - heart and lung capacity.

catching - this skill involves the use of the hands to stop or grasp an airborne object such as a ball.

cephalocaudal development - developing control of the body from the head and proceeding down to the lower limbs.

climbing - involves the use of both hands and feet, which work together through homolateral or contralateral movements to move a child up and/or over an object.

contraindicated - not recommended.

contralateral action - this action occurs in such movements as creeping and climbing. The arms and legs move in opposite directions to each other.

cooperative games - a game or activity where the group works together towards one common goal.

cooperative play - where children work together to organize an activity or game.

corralling - the child's first attempts at reaching for an object with their hands.

crawling - the child is in the prone position with the stomach flat on the floor and uses his arms to pull himself along.

creative dance - a choreographed or arranged combination of creative movements.

creeping - this action usually follows the skill of crawling. The child is on hands and knees with the torso off the ground and uses either a homolateral or contralateral action to move the body.

cruise - the child is in an upright position and holding onto an object while moving the feet along in a sideways movement.

developmental direction - the predetermined sequence of motor development that all normal human beings go through.

differentiation - refinement of motor tasks.

directional awareness - it is an understanding that there are two sides to the body. It is also the ability to move the body in different directions.

dynamic balance - adjusting one's balance while the body is in motion.

eye-foot coordination - the processing of information received through the eyes and translated by the brain to send a message to the foot or feet.

eye-hand coordination - the processing of information received by the eye and translated or reacted upon by the hand or hands.

equilibrium - maintaining one's balance.

external stimuli - stimuli from the environment.

fine motor skill - the ability to coordinate the small muscles, i.e., hand and foot control.

fine motor manipulation - use of hands and fingers in holding or manoeuvring an object.

flexibility - the range of motion in a joint.

fundamental movements - controlled movements that form the basis for activities of daily living as well as all sports and advanced movement skills.

fundamental skill - a basic motor skill such as locomotion, nonlocomotion, or manipulation.

functional play - play that involves repetitive motor actions.

gross motor manipulation - involves the use of large muscle groups, the various limbs of the body, and an object.

gross motor skills - these skills involve the use of the larger muscles and limbs of the body.

group games - involve the active participation of the entire group of children.

guided fantasy - storytelling with the goal of provoking imagery and becoming in touch with one's inner feelings.

homolateral action - this action involves the arm and leg on the same side of the body moving in synchrony. This action can be observed in creeping and climbing.

hopping - the child takes off and lands on the same foot.

imagery - internal visualization of an idea or feeling.

jumping - the child takes off and lands on two feet.

kicking - the child maintains balance on one leg while the other leg is lifted off the ground to impart force onto an object.

knowledge base - the foundation of existing knowledge. This changes as new knowledge is acquired.

kinaesthesis - perceptual process of interpreting stimuli without the use of visual cues.

leaping - the child takes off on one foot and lands on the opposite foot.

locomotor skills - moving the body from one point in space to another.

manipulation - involves some form of control or adjustment of an object with a body part, usually the hands and feet.

muscular endurance - the ability of a muscle or muscle group to continuously repeat actions.

muscular strength - the ability to exert force to an object with a muscle or muscle group.

motor development - the increase in motor control that individuals have over their bodies.

motor refinement - the fine tuning and improvement of motor skills.

nonlocomotor skills - includes nonmanipulative movements that occur in one spot such as twisting or bending.

object permanence - the realization that an object still exists, even when it can no longer be seen.

ontogenetic - development of an individual organism.

parachute - a nylon piece of equipment that is circular in design and varies in size and dimension.

perceptual motor development - involves monitoring and interpreting sensory data and responding to this data through movement.

phylogenetic - evolutionary development of an organism.

physical fitness - level of one's health and well-being.

prone position - lying on the stomach or front part of the body.

proximodistal development - development of control of the body from the centre outwards.

reaching - the child uses manipulation skills and eye-hand coordination to reach for objects.

reaction time - the time it takes to respond to an action.

releasing - the child has developed the fine motor skills that allow him to let go of an object that he has been holding.

reflex - involuntary movement caused by a stimulus.

repetitive play - repeating a movement or task over and over in order to learn through motor experience.

rudimentary movement -the beginning of voluntary actions and controlled movements.

running - looks like fast walking with a flight phase between the steps.

skipping - is a combination of a step and a hop with the feet alternating.

spatial awareness -awareness of personal space and room space.

spontaneous play - play that is self initiated and unrehearsed.

stability - the individual's ability to maintain his balance.

static balance - movements that occur in one spot, while the body is still. (nonlocomotor movements)

striking - a moving or stationary object is projected into space through the application of force. This application of force is carried out by either a body part or an implement that is used as an extension of the body.

subcortically controlled - movement patterns that are controlled by the lower part of the brain.

supine position - lying on the back.

tactile perception - involves the sense of touch.

temporal awareness - internal awareness of a time structure.

throwing - involves either one or both hands and an object. The child uses the hands to propel an object away from the body.

torso - the trunk of the body.

transference - the ability to use a skill learned through one action to facilitate the achievement of another action.

tracking - the visual interception of a moving object.

trapping - any part of the body can be used to trap an object.

visual perception - information received through the sense of sight.

walking -upright locomotion, weight is transferred from one foot to the other. Mature pattern involves heel-toe action.

INDEX

READER REPLY CARD

We are interested in your reaction to *Moving to Learn* by Nyisztor and Stelzer Rudick. You can help us to improve this book in future editions by completing this questionnaire.

1. What was your reason for using this book?
   ☐ university course   ☐ continuing education course   ☐ personal interest
   ☐ college course   ☐ professional development   ☐ other _____

2. If you are a student, please identify your school and the course in which you used this book.

3. Which chapters or parts of this book did you use? Which did you omit?

4. What did you like best about this book? What did you like least?

5. Please identify any topics you think should be added to future editions.

6. Please add any comments or suggestions.

7. May we contact you for further information?

   NAME: _____
   ADDRESS: _____
             _____
   PHONE: _____

(fold here and tape shut)

MAIL  POSTE

Canada Post Corporation / Société canadienne des postes

Postage paid
If mailed in Canada

Port payé
si posté au Canada

**Business
Reply**

**Réponse
d'affaires**

0116870399   01

0116870399-M8Z4X6-BR01

Heather McWhinney
Publisher, College Division
HARCOURT BRACE & COMPANY, CANADA
55 HORNER AVENUE
TORONTO, ONTARIO
M8Z 9Z9